Budget Prepper Guide

Pete Thorsen

**Formerly Published
Under the Pen Name
Jack Forester**

Originally Released

On Kindle March 2014

In Print in October 2016

Updated January 2018

Table of Contents

1. Overview

The objective of this guide is not to dictate a list of things to do or to buy but more to offer suggestions and to get you thinking about aspects of prepping and 'what if' scenarios that might affect you personally and what you could do now ahead of time to make it easier for yourself and your family later when or if something happens. This is written more like a conversation rather than a manual in the hope that you might find it easier to read.

Everyone has different needs, and everyone is unique. Each of us has different surroundings. Some are single; some are married, some have kids, some have a house, some an apartment – the list of things different about each of us is endless.

So naturally, the things we want to do to prepare are way different. Some things are the same for each of us. We all must drink, eat, and sleep. Hence the headings on the chapters and they are mostly in order of importance. Like water is number one, maybe. Water might not be number one if you are outside in ten degrees below zero weather with the wind blowing. Then it would be shelter. Or if you are on the street and three guys with machetes and mean looks are advancing on you. Then a drink of water is the last thing on your mind.

What kind of disaster to prepare for? Again that is different for different people. If you live in Iowa, you don't have to worry about a hurricane but maybe a blizzard. In Florida, it would be the opposite, and in New York, it could be both. If you lose your job and cannot find another, it is a disaster and your preps would certainly come in handy. An economic disaster seems to be looming over the nation (almost every nation right now) and could happen at most any time, or maybe never.

Natural disasters are many in number and can happen anywhere and anytime, some without any warning at all. No matter what disaster you prepare for you still need to drink, eat, sleep, and be secure.

Prepping on a tight budget can be fun and rewarding if you get into it. Finding that special item at a yard sale for a way low price can be both exciting and rewarding. Think about how many things can be repurposed. Be a savvy shopper. Watch the prices and look for sales, so you know what is really a good deal and what is not. When it is a good sale on something you always use, then stock up.

Haunt the thrift stores and second-hand shops. Watch Craigslist for bargains and for yard sales. Yard sales are your best friend. Some things you will want to buy new but many things are just as good after they are used. That forty-year-old cast iron fry pan is just as good (or better) now than it was when it was brand new. With most things, it is best to buy quality even if it is used instead of new.

Even if something is cheap don't buy it unless you have a use for it. Make a want list of things to keep an eye out for at yard sales, so you don't forget. If an item has multiple uses that is all the better and makes it more valuable to you.

Make sure you know how to use everything you buy, and I mean everything, including food. Once you buy something, use it until you are comfortable in its use. If that means wearing it out or using it up so be it. Buy another when you are done testing and learning. Many items can sometimes be purchased cheaper on eBay (both new and used) or other online stores.

Dollar stores seem like a good place to pick up cheap stuff. How can you go wrong if everything is only a dollar? Like any shopping, it is buyer beware. Yes, there are maybe some bargains on useful items that can be found at a dollar store, but often things can actually be found cheaper elsewhere. Also quality is often an issue at these stores. So I say yes, definitely shop through a dollar store once in a while but just be careful what you buy there.

Throughout this guide I may occasionally mention a certain brand item or a certain business but please note that I am not promoting that item or business. I am only pointing something out and maybe a place to start looking for an item that you may think about buying (or something similar in possibly a different brand or style).

No one can walk you through every possible scenario you might encounter. That is obviously impossible. All I can do with this book is to get you thinking of some things ahead of time and preparing for some of them. Thinking is the always the key to survival. And when possible do the thinking now instead of during any disaster.

And none of us can prepare for everything. Or be completely prepared for even one thing. But we can all get some preparations ready to help us through many different scenarios. And we can all think, that is the key element in every single step of prepping and in any survival situation.

Some key parts of getting prepared can cost nothing. Exercise is one, and it is a **very** important one. Everyone can exercise. I don't care what your medical condition is you can still exercise some. If you have no legs, then exercise your arms. No, you don't start by trying to do a hundred push-ups or trying to run ten miles. You start where you start, whether you can do five push-ups or twenty-five. And/or you jog, or you run, or you walk, or you do jumping jacks. Unless you are in a wheelchair, then your exercises should mean getting off your butt. And no you do not have to buy some expensive piece of exercise equipment.

Running, biking, jogging, and/or walking have another bonus and that is getting to know your neighborhood. Whether it is in the city or in the country. You can drive down the same street every day on the way to work, but if you walk it, you will see things that you never noticed while you were driving.

And that is another prep item you can do that is free. And that item is you learn to **notice** things, not just see them. You see that house has two dogs in the backyard. But you notice that those dogs are big Rottweilers, and you make a mental note that you should not cut through his backyard at night, ever.

So as you read through this guide remember everything that is said within you will have to modify to fit your own personal situation and needs. I will touch on many different things in this guide, but for many things, you will need additional information on it to do a good job. With a Kindle (or Kindle app) you can get free books all the time on a wide range of subjects. One place you can find these free books is at http://www.freereadfeed.com. This site has a huge list of free kindle books that change daily. Free is an excellent price! Check out that site off and on. The books change almost every day, and there are fiction and non-fiction books. Books on almost everything you can think of reading.

One of the things that has the most impact on your future survival is the most difficult to do anything about – your location. If you are a renter, it might be possible to get yourself to a better location (for survival) without too much additional cost.

If you own your home or you and the bank together own your home then moving is a very big deal and could very easily be cost prohibitive. Many are underwater on their home mortgages and are stuck where they are for now. Most people just have to make do with where they are living right now and make what improvements they can afford that can improve their chances of survival there. This might be a low-cost thing like planting a garden or reading some free books from the local library.

And if you do decide you want to start prepping and storing some stuff, you do not have to do it all at once. Do **not** take out a loan or use credit card debt to prep. Instead when you are shopping just maybe buy two of some things you use instead of just one. There is nothing wrong with starting slow. Actually that is the best way. Knowledge is something you can very often prep for free and is maybe the most vital prep item you will ever have anyway.

Knowledge and skills are things to always work on as much as possible. Much can be done at little or no cost. The local library is full of books and information. If you have internet access, then free E-book downloads were already mentioned, but there are also you-tube videos. You can watch these videos on almost everything to get some valuable additional knowledge. But you do have to be careful. While the internet is full of truthful knowledge, it is also full of lies and deceitful information. Like with everything else a person has to be careful and try to research everything to see if what you are reading is true or not. And remember that many things are not really either true or false but instead are opinions. For every opinion, there is always another that is a counter-opinion. Both can be true depending on how you look at things. Things like saying a Ford is the best car is just an opinion. Not true or untrue but instead just an opinion.

2. Water

It should be obvious to everyone that water is essential for life. It should be the first thing on your agenda.   Prepping water is cheap but hard to do. Water is bulky and heavy. Water is easily contaminated. We need water basically every day, and it is used for more than just drinking. The average US citizen uses roughly a hundred gallons of water per day for drinking, washing, flushing, and other uses.

We drink some, we cook with some, we wash with some, we flush with some, and we use it in many ways throughout the day, every single day. To just stay alive most agree you may need to drink one half to one gallon of water per day, or more, every day.

Many have experienced lack of water when there was a power outage. No matter if you live in the country or the city no electric power also means no water 99 percent of the time. Often there is a 'grace period' because of stored water in the city water towers (or in a home cistern). Those water towers in cities and towns store water and dispense it the same for a while without power until the tank is empty.

Especially in the eastern half of the United States, most people live reasonably close to a permanent surface water supply; a lake, a river, a creek, or a pond. The downside is surface water like that is usually contaminated with many things, both organic and inorganic.

Tiny living things that you can not see live in most surface water. Boiling the water for a few minutes can kill these things (like bacteria and viruses). Some can be killed by straining the water through a cloth or a filter to get it mostly clear then putting the water in a clear plastic bottle or a clear bag (like a ziplock bag) and exposing it to the sun. The UV radiation from the sun will kill those little living organisms (in theory).

If you drink the water without killing the living stuff in that water, you will likely end up with dysentery or diarrhea which is not fun in the best of times and certainly to be avoided in the worst of times during a disaster and can even turn deadly by dehydrating you.

There are many portable and non-portable water filters available and many that you can make on your own. Few remove viruses which are very small and pass right through most water filters. Some have silver screen in the filter that for a time will kill the viruses. There is no way for you to know when that killing action stops and the viruses are just passing through the filter still alive.

My advice is to filter your water and then boil it if at all possible. City water usually has chlorine put into the water to kill the bad stuff. You can also do this same thing yourself with common unscented chlorine bleach. Ten to twenty drops of bleach in a gallon of water should kill the bad stuff living in the water.

Oops, use too much chlorine? That's okay; chlorine dissipates quickly in water if it is exposed to the air. To speed up this dissipation process just pour some of that water into a drinking glass and then pour it back and forth into another glass a few times, which will remove much of the taste and odor of the chlorine through oxygenation.

You can also use the chlorine tablets (shock) or liquid chlorine that you have for your pool. Read the ingredients to make sure it does not have other stuff mixed with the chlorine (Sodium hypochlorite) (caution; the pool stuff is way more concentrated than simple bleach). Liquid chlorine (like bleach) weakens over time. The pool tablets do not if stored sealed. Remember chlorine basically kills all living organisms (including you) so use some caution. But almost everyone in this country using city water drinks water that has been treated with chlorine every single day of their lives.

Many people buy water purification tablets that can be found in the camping section of many stores, even at Walmart. These are little pills that can be stored for a long time and are clearly marked as how much to use for how much water. These pills are usually iodine tablets (same as the military uses). These are safe and easy to use and easy to carry. They are relatively cheap but are meant for emergency use only, not for extended periods.

What about the old days when everyone just drank right out of the creeks? You can still do that but you may face a long uncomfortable period of time before your body gets accustomed to this unfiltered and unclean water and of course, there is also has the unfortunate possibility that the unfiltered water may kill you. People that have gotten Giardia from drinking surface water can tell you that it is no fun at all and requires a trip to the doctor.

Water now may also contain many different pollutants. Some of these can be easily filtered out with water filters and some can not. The list of these possible contaminants would be very long and not mean much to most people. Plus there is no way for you to know what is in that water in the creek without sending the water in to be tested. My advice for what its worth, is in an emergency situation filter and/or boil the water and drink it if you are thirsty.

Nature cleans water all the time. Through distillation where water evaporates and then falls to earth as pretty clean rain water. Also through infusing the water with oxygen, which kills many organisms. Nature puts the oxygen in the water by using waterfalls and rushing, splashing water in fast moving streams and rivers.

And nature's favorite method of cleaning water is through natural filtration. When water seeps through the earth, it gets cleaned of most contaminates. That is why we can drink water directly from a well.

Many people make simple sand water filters that do a pretty good job of removing particulate matter from water. There are many ways to make a simple sand filter, and the key thing is to make the dirty water seep through a bunch of sand before the water runs out the bottom of your 'filter' as clean water.

One method uses two similar five-gallon buckets. Punch small holes into the bottom of one bucket (this will be your top bucket). Lay a layer of clean felt, or flattened coffee filters (they can overlap that's fine), or a couple of layers of cloth to completely cover the bottom of the pail with the small holes in the bottom. If your filter material comes up the sides of the bucket some that is just fine.

Next, fill this bucket with clean fine sand. Children's play sand can be purchased for this use. Or fine, clean sand from a creek or lakeshore could be used. Before putting this sand into the filter bucket mix up some chlorine water (this could be mixed a little strong because you will not be drinking this water). Pour the chlorine water in with the clean sand and mix or agitate some, so the chlorine has a chance to make contact with all the sand.

Then take this now mostly sterile sand and put in your filter bucket. Next, you can set the filter bucket into the other cleaned five-gallon bucket. Now water dumped into the top bucket will slowly be filtered by the sand and exit as relatively clean water into the bottom bucket. To get the clean water just pull the buckets apart and dump the clean water from the bottom bucket into any clean container. Or drill a hole near the bottom of the lower bucket and attach a hose for continuous use with the filtered water running out of the hose.

This water can then be boiled and used for drinking. The sand should filter out most items suspended in the dirty water. It will do nothing for the taste and will not filter out any small living organisms, hence the need to boil before drinking.

You can capture rainwater to drink. While the rainwater itself is likely just fine to drink, by the time you capture it and get into a container it may become contaminated. Many capture rainwater using rain gutters from their roof and catch it from the downspout. This is fine but remember you are in effect washing everything that may be on your roof or in your gutters and putting it into your water container. One of the things this would likely include would be bird droppings and also include various live and dead insects along with anything else that the wind blew into the gutters.

So this captured rainwater should also be filtered. Maybe just run it through that sand filter that you just made would be enough. Or even just filter it through a coffee filter to at least get out the chunks. It all depends on just how thirsty you are as to what you will accept as clean enough to drink. Catching rainwater is certainly a viable idea and can be done almost anywhere. Even in an apartment in the middle of a large city, a window can be opened and rainwater captured with a piece of plastic at least to some extent to provide some additional water.

There are many different water filters that you can purchase for emergency use. These usually will say how small of particles they will filter. Commonly these will filter out particles as small as .2 microns, and some will take out even smaller particles. The cost of these filters varies greatly. Starting at about fifteen dollars and going up from there. For an emergency, a small filter like the Sawyer Mini water filter is available many places (including Walmart) and sells for about twenty bucks. It might be a low-cost possibility for many people on a budget that want something for emergencies.

A warning about most water filters- - that smelly pond water after being filtered will still smell and taste like pond water. It might very well be safe to drink but still smell and taste bad. You can cover that taste by adding drink packets available at most grocery stores if you wish.   Also boiling the water can often make it taste better. Multi-stage water filters that include a carbon filter will make the water better tasting.

Well Options

Years ago people would hand dig wells and get the relatively clean water out with a bucket on a rope. This still works today just like it did a thousand years ago. This open type well easily lets many things fall into the well water (sometimes relatively nasty things).

If the underground water level is within twenty-five feet of the surface, we can sometimes pound a pipe down and suck the water up with a simple suction pump, either an electric or hand pump. This is called a shallow well and is an option in many places in the United States but might not be a legal well in some locations for a residence. This is often the type well you see in old pictures with a hand pump next to the kitchen sink.

In the country now most homes (and towns) have a deep well (often 50 feet to 500 feet deep) that has an electric pump that sits submerged in the water near the bottom of the well. Obviously, with no electric power, it means no water can be pumped from the well.

There are options, of course, to get water from that well without using the power grid. The easy method is to use a generator big enough to power the existing pump and get the water just like when the electric grid is turned on. This is the easiest, simplest method and possibly the least expensive option. This requires buying a large enough generator and having enough fuel to run it whenever you want water. This is maybe the best option for many people that want a backup water supply.

A generator big enough to run your pump may cost at least $500 and likely more plus the cost of the fuel. The added benefit would be having the electricity also available for other uses at the same time, like running your freezer or other electric items when the grid power is off.

The next option is a solar powered pump that replaces your old electric pump, and you use it all the time. Or a solar pump that is hooked up in tandem with your existing well pump in the same well (this is not always possible). A solar setup may cost over two thousand dollars, but there are countless options available in solar.

The next option is a hand pump that can sometimes be used alongside the existing electric pump but is not tied into the water pipes leading to your house. When you want water, you take your bucket to the hand pump and pump the bucket full then carry it back to the house.

Some wells are too deep to use a hand pump. Sometimes a hand pump cannot be installed and used at the same time a standard submersible pump is in place and being used. And a good deep well hand pump can easily cost a thousand dollars by the time you get it in (though there are some available for substantially less that can sometimes be used).

Another option is a windmill. While still manufactured these are now seldom installed. I think the only company that still makes these is Aermotor.

There is also something called a well bucket that can sometimes be used to get water out of a standard deep well in an emergency. This is basically just a long skinny bucket (usually a piece of plastic pipe with a special end) that is lowered down the well by hand or by winch/windlass and then pulled back up full of water. This is very similar in operation as the old hand dug wells that used a standard bucket on a rope.

Using a well bucket in a well usually means removing the existing pump and pipes from the well so the bucket can be lowered all the way down to the water level. Keep in mind that your deep well might be hundreds of feet deep so you would need a very long rope and it would be a slow process to lift that bucket up all that distance. But still, a viable method to get clean drinking water in an emergency situation.

Getting water in a grid-down emergency situation is seldom going to be easy. Even getting water from a nearby surface water source is a lot of work. Water is heavy. About eight pounds for each gallon. About two or three gallons just to flush the toilet which means about twenty pounds of water per flush. Walking a quarter mile to the nearby creek and carrying the heavy water back to your house uses a lot of valuable calories and requires a fair amount of strength and stamina just to accomplish and if that is your only water source, you would need to carry a lot of water for a family of four to survive. If that is your planned water source in an emergency, then I would suggest buying a wagon or cart of some kind to make the job much easier. Also, you would want to have lids for the pails you use so your valuable water does not all splash out on the trip home.

Storing water

If you have a little room available you can think about storing water. Do not store any water in old plastic milk containers or similar water containers as the thin opaque plastic jugs are made for short-term use only and will sometimes fail (leak or burst open) if used for longer-term storage. To me, this is just not worth the risk. The hard clear plastic containers that juice often comes in work much better just because they are heavier duty (and still free).

If you are on a 'city' water supply, your water already contains some chlorine, so it is ready for long-term storage. If you use well water a couple of drops of unscented bleach in each container will make the water last longer. Some buy those big fifty-five-gallon plastic barrels (often blue) to store larger quantities of water. These can be purchased new or used but make sure they are made of food grade plastic if you use them for drinking water.

If you get used barrels make sure they never contained any kind of toxic chemicals. Buying used barrels from a food prep company that got liquid food additives in them should be safe. If buying used barrels smell the inside of the barrel before you purchase. Any odor inside the barrel will help you know what was in the barrel previously. Note that these odors are often very difficult to remove and may transfer to the water you store in them.

If you decide to use large containers like the fifty-five gallon barrels or a larger container make sure you also have a plan to get the water out of those containers easily. The barrels can be laid horizontal on racks, and you can use a simple spigot. Or upright and use a siphon hose or a pump. Also, remember that a full barrel will weigh about four hundred and fifty pounds or so. Make sure it is sitting on something very solid that will withstand that weight.

Most homes already have 30 to 50 gallons of potable water stored in the water heater that can be used in any emergency. It even has a handy drain on the bottom. If you use this water out of the water heater make sure you shut off the gas or electric to the water heater first.

The water heater will drain much better if you open a hot water tap somewhere in the house first. If you live in an apartment building, I would try to find out where the apartments' water heaters are (just in case) so you could access this stored water if necessary.

Stored water should last six months to a year after that it may still be fine, but it is always a good idea to rotate any water that is stored if at all possible.

Those of you that live in the frozen north will have a tougher time trying to store water or carry water in the winter. Drinking water is WAY better than eating snow. You do have the advantage of having all that potable water stored in a solid white state outside but melt this before use. When traveling in very cold weather keep a water bottle under your jacket, so it does not freeze for you to drink.

If you live near a body of water and your emergency plan is to haul water from that source to your house that is a fine idea. But remember that water is quite heavy & bulky, and hauling water gets old fast. Have a plan on how you will move this water, preferably one that does not require you to physically carry that water. A wagon, a wheelbarrow, or most anything with wheels would be a good idea.

If you live in the desert or warm southern states, you already know that you will require a lot of water to keep you hydrated in the summer. Don't compare how much you drink while in the air conditioning setting at a desk or in front of a TV with how much water you will need when hiking outside in the sun carrying a pack or working outside in the sun all day. When I hike in the summer here, it is not uncommon for me to drink a pint to a quart an hour.

Yes, you can push yourself for a time without any water but know your limits if you try that. If necessary work or walk at night if possible to conserve water.

Some homes use a water cistern to hold water. This is commonly just a large cement or plastic tank that holds water for the home's use.

I freely admit that I do not store any water (except in the water heater) at this time. But we do have our own well and a generator large enough to power the well pump and other items at same time. We also store some extra fuel for the generator. We did also add a rain water catchment system to use for the garden.

Were my situation different I would likely store an amount of water (and I still might). Like everything else about prepping we all have to decide what we want to stock up on and we all have different situations and space considerations.

If you have pets or livestock plan ahead for what you will do about water for them. They can drink right out of a river or a pond or even a mud puddle. So while their water supply may be easier, you still have to think about it before something happens.

If you have a swimming pool, you already have a large supply of water. If you are forewarned about a lack of a water supply, you can buy small kids pools and set them up and fill them ahead of time. Even the smallest kiddie pool often holds fifty gallons of water or more.

In a pinch, these can be set up indoors, so you have more control over who gets the water and keep it cleaner and handier. An outdoor pool will bring all the neighbors over to get water from you, which would be fine in a short-term situation but might be a big problem in a long-term scenario. Just like food, in a long-term situation, potable water will be in high demand and in short supply. Anyone with a working well could give away or barter away the clean water to others.

An early prepping investment might be a quality water filter. There are hundreds from which to choose. Some are portable like for backpackers, and some are larger more permanent ones that sit on the counter. The Brita type water filters for the kitchen are not made to change pond water into potable drinking water.

Usually, the water filters that you want to look at will be in the camping section. Commonly they filter down to about point two microns, and some are washable, and others require you to occasionally change the inner filter. Again some are made to kill viruses, and most are not. Viruses are too small to filter out.

You can also store juice and soda and sports drinks, and that is fine and can be used as a treat for anyone to help boost morale.

Also filtered water while it might be perfectly safe to drink might still taste like a well-used sock. Powdered drink mix packets can be stored and used to enhance the taste of filtered water or used as a treat for kids or adults. Sometimes these powdered drink mixes also provide some nutrients besides just flavor.

Good filters do not have to cost hundreds of dollars. The Sawyer Mini Filter does up to 100,000 gallons of water, filters down to .1 micron, is very compact, and costs about $20.

The Life Straw is another very inexpensive personal filter. They are popular for inclusion in a Bug Out Bag and cost $15 to $20.

There are many good filters out there for sale. Some have carbon inside the filters that make the filtered water taste much better. The carbon filters have to be occasionally changed. Some contain a silver screen to help kill viruses. Do some research and pick up a couple of water filters as soon as you can afford one. Again most Walmart stores stock them or most sporting good stores. Or the internet is full of choices.

Many disasters are short-lived things. The blizzard blows over and the roads open again, the hurricane only lasts a couple of days and then clean up begins, the tornado is gone in less than a minute or two and again clean up can start. But even in a short-term disaster, you will need water to survive. If we have to go a week without food most of us will emerge looking trimmer and better. A week without water and we will all be dead.

There is one thing to always keep in mind about prepping and getting ready for some kind of disaster situation…………

Water is a big deal; have a plan for it.

A water plan for both at home and if you have to ever bug out.

3. Food

Food storage is very important, and thoughts on food storage vary widely. Some people store buckets of wheat, corn, beans, and rice. For many people, they would only know what to do with maybe the rice. With the prepper/survivalist fad right now many companies are selling LTS food. Long-Term Storage food.

Some are just as is, so to speak, like beans or wheat. Some are dehydrated, and some are freeze dried. And of course, some is your standard canned goods. Advice commonly given is 'store what you eat and eat what you store.' That is very sound advice. What they mean is buy stuff that you normally eat and then always eat the oldest item first, so you rotate your stored food supply just with your normal diet.

The great thing about storing food for survival is that it is easy to start and not expensive. Cans of vegetables can often be purchased on sale for about fifty cents per can. Or canned tuna or canned chicken is often only around a dollar per can. Most people have an extra buck so they could buy two cans for storage. You don't have to buy a whole year's supply all at once. You buy a little extra each week. Like when you are planning on eating spaghetti soon so you buy a box of the pasta, just buy an extra box. Pasta has a long storage life and it is very reasonable to purchase. Start slow and just buy extra of the regular foods you always buy.

So if you eat canned green beans and you buy twenty cans when it is on sale then store it with the oldest cans to the front, so that is what you use first. And the next time they are on sale again buy more but put the new cans in back behind the older cans. This way you rotate your stock of food. And you are only storing food that you will actually eat.

Canned items can often be eaten right out of the can without any further cooking, a big plus in an emergency situation. Canned goods often contain liquid that can extend your stored water supply, another bonus. But if you are not going to eat it don't buy it. So don't buy canned oysters or something if you would never eat it or if you can not eat it due to an allergy. Only buy what you will eat. Also, buy an extra non-electric can opener (though the trend in canned goods has been to gradually change over to pop-top cans).

Many people don't realize that many items can be stored a long time. Milk can be stored in the cupboard if it is 'shelf stable milk' and can be stored for a year or more that way. If nothing else it is handy to have on hand when you run out of the regular milk. This is found in grocery stores next to evaporated milk and condensed milk (also good storage items). It is just regular milk that is 'super pasteurized' so most people can not tell the difference from standard milk (I can't, and I often use it when I run out of regular milk or when I rotate my stock). This shelf stable milk is usually found in one-quart cartons. A quick look at the expiration date will show you that it is made to store up to a year or more and with no refrigeration needed (and likely will store twice that long with no problems).

Eggs can be bought that are dehydrated or freeze-dried and can last a long time (usually about ten years). Dried butter and cheese can be stored a long time. But stored items don't always have to be something that can be stored for ten years either. Even if it is something that lasts only a year that is fine as long as it is something that you normally eat, just rotate your stock as you eat it.

Canned goods (and most foods) commonly last much, much longer than the 'expiration date.' Companies are required to put on an expiration date, and then occasionally their product is tested by the government to see if it is still good at that point. The company picks the date, and it is to their advantage to shorten the date considerably. Let's say you tested your product and it commonly lasts three years or more. But just to be on the safe side, you mark it as expires in one year (or even less). That way when the government does test your product, there is no chance of them ever finding a bad one. Also, people commonly throw out food that is past the expiration date and just buy more. This is another reason for companies to shorten expiration dates just so they can sell more.

You can can your own food. Including even things like butter and meat. Many items can be canned at home and last a long time that way (think years). Most pressure canners come with a canning guide, or a canning book can often be found next to the canning supplies in stores and purchased there. With a pressure canner, jars, and some lids you can store meat without freezing it. A big plus if there is no power. Home canned food can easily last for way more than a year; actually maybe more than ten years. Just keep in mind that most lids are a one-time use thing so store a lot of them (they're cheap). One company does sell re-usable plastic canning lids (tattler lids).

Ramen is a very cheap food (ask most any poor college kid). It doesn't taste bad, stores pretty good, cooks fast and easy. It is often high in salt content though. I don't recommend that you plan on living on ramen because it is so cheap but it seems logical to include some in your preps. If nothing else it can be what you might hand out to beggars that come to your door. If they see all you have is ramen they will know you don't have much. But if you are starving some ramen would be like a feast.

Don't buy a five-gallon bucket of lima beans if you don't eat lima beans. Don't buy a bucket of wheat if you don't know what to do with it (do you have a grain mill?). One common long-term storage food is white rice. Yes, brown rice is maybe better for you but does not store as long. Rice is easy to fix and relatively fast to fix. It can be added to many other things to make a more filling meal. And it is readily available and pretty cheap to buy. Walmart has twenty pounds of rice for about ten bucks. Seal it up good, and it will store for many years (10 to 20 years or even more).

Rice is also something that many of us already commonly eat. The directions for cooking rice is - - combine rice with double the amount of water (example ½ cup rice and 1 cup water), boil for fifteen minutes, let stand without heat for five minutes, then eat. There is a product called Minute rice or Quick rice. This is precooked and then dehydrated rice. Just add an equal amount of boiling water to the rice, let stand for a minute and eat. Quicker and easier but this product does not store as long as regular rice but is still a viable option to keep on hand or in your BOB. Remember rice can be eaten by itself or countless things can be combined with it.

Many people buy 'oxygen absorber packets' to put in their sealed LTS food to make it last even longer. Some also include water absorbing desiccant packs. Either or both of these will likely lengthen storage times but whether they are worth the extra money spent on them is everyone's choice. If you regularly rotate your food stocks, I feel they might not be needed, but then again they are not that expensive.

Don't have a lot of room to store stuff because you live in a small apartment? Be ingenious and hide it in plain sight. Take the legs off your coffee table and set the table on top of five-gallon buckets full of food or water. Then cover with a tablecloth that hangs low enough to cover everything. Store food under the bed or in the back of your closet. Stored food is a valuable asset that could save your life. Food is relatively cheap so almost anyone can at least store some for emergencies.

Don't plan on 'living off the land' but you could plan on supplementing your stored food when possible with whatever fresh food you might be able to gather. Many things are found even in towns and cities. Dandelion greens are good to eat and found almost everywhere. Those pigeons that are in the park are very good eating (cook them and add some rice for a very good meal). Squirrels are found in city parks almost everywhere and are quite tasty.

Snare that stray cat. Skin it before your wife sees what it is and then tell her it is a rabbit. Save the guts out of the dead cat and use that for bait for fishing or bait to trap other animals. If it moves the chances are that you can eat it and protein is vital for survival. See those Robins in the front yard, use your slingshot that is quiet and nab a couple. Cook them and add some rice for a nice meal! (Note it is not legal to kill songbirds like that Robin. But if it is a survival situation then you do what you must to survive).

Buy a book on edible plants in your area with good pictures. Then buy another one, so you have more pictures and a second opinion. Many wild things are edible, but some are not. Know what you are about to eat before you sink your teeth into it. If you are not sure let your mother-in-law try it first or else just pass it by. Books on foraging, edible plants, and plant identification will store forever and supply an unending source of food for you and your family. The key to finding and eating wild plants is to do so well ahead of the time when your life might depend on those wild foods.

Buy the books now and then gather plants on your walks to try out at home. Start slow and only eat small portions at first until you know if your body can tolerate certain plants. Gradually build up your knowledge on edible plants until you know what is not only edible but also tasty. Also, you can learn where to look for certain plants. This knowledge will not happen overnight but will be a gradual process so start now when finding these wild plants is not a matter of life and death. Also, different seasons of the year means totally different plants to look for and often which different parts of the plants to gather. Some plants have to be cooked, and some can be eaten raw. There is much to learn about foraging so start that learning process NOW!

Old vacant places may have fruit trees or nut trees that you can harvest when in season. Most locations in the United States have some form of oak trees that you can harvest the acorns from in the fall. These can be crushed or ground into a meal and eaten different ways but know that you have to soak them first enough to remove the tannins or they will make you sick.

Soak the acorns in plain water for a couple of hours then change the water and soak again. You might have to change the water two or more times. Before soaking them taste an acorn and it will be bitter. After soaking taste again and it will have a nice nutty taste or if still bitter just soak again in more fresh water and re-taste. The bitter taste is the excess tannins found in this otherwise tasty and nut.

Foraging plants for food is fine but these plants often have little nutritional value and few calories. In many cases the energy used to find the wild plants might consume more calories than you get from what you find and eat. A net loss of calories does you no good. Nuts (like acorns) and berries usually are very good sources of calories.

When you shoot that stray dog, be neighborly and share the meat with your neighbor. Besides, it will very likely spoil before you could eat it all anyway. Remember if it flies, walks, or crawls it is likely edible and full of protein.

Also, keep in mind that if there is no electric, there will be no refrigerator or freezer to store that meat. And how are you going to be cooking everything? Plan ahead. If you have an all-electric house how will you cook with no electricity? Even if you have natural gas (city gas) that will likely stop flowing to your house if the power is down for awhile, so then what?

Do you have a propane gas grill with extra propane tanks? That will work. But if the neighbor sees you cooking on the grill (or smells you cooking up some cat (BBQ'ed cat, mmm!)) he'll be hungry and come over to eat your food.

A propane camp stove can be used inside your house to cook on, in private and in comfort. Remember to have extra fuel on hand for it. Yes, you can always cook outside with a campfire (or inside with a fireplace or wood stove). But you will need firewood, and the smoke will show everyone nearby that supper is cooking!

Many are afraid to use a camp stove inside their homes because they will be asphyxiated by the fumes or it will use up all the oxygen in the room, and everyone will die. Hogwash!

Using a propane camp stove for cooking your supper inside will not cause any harmful effects. You will use it for ten to thirty minutes and eat a nice meal and suffer no ill effects. This is different than using it for heat where the stove burns for many, many hours at a time. Remember that maybe roughly half of the homes in the nation use unvented gas kitchen stoves that are either propane or natural gas. All of these stoves are the same as a propane camp stove.

Another possibility is cooking with a solar oven. This is basically just a box with a glass front that you set in the sun to absorb the sun's heat. There are many different solar ovens that you can buy or many plans and videos online that show you how to make your own. It can be as simple as a cardboard box with aluminum foil wings to direct the sun into the box and onto the dark pan setting inside that box. Using the sun to cook your meals or purify water is an excellent idea. But plan ahead and build or buy one now and test it to know how to use it in an emergency.

And that brings us to sharing your food.

Sharing food

So you have all that food stored up for your family and all your neighbors' have is a salt shaker and a fork. Do you share? This is a personal question and circumstances could easily change your answer. If you have plenty of food and the emergency situation is for sure just a temporary one, then the likely logical answer is to share with your friends and neighbors.

But what if the situation is very likely to be long-term of a month or possibly even a year? In any bad situation, there will be beggars just like there are now only they will be in larger numbers and much more desperate. And desperate people do desperate things.

In the long-term situation if you share your food with a beggar and he/she/they move on they will return when they need food again. And if another person asks them where they got that food they will say your house. Soon your house will be the local soup kitchen and your stored food that could have lasted your family of four for a year is now almost gone because instead of feeding just the four of you are instead feeding ten or twenty beggars or even more.

Now you tell all of them the food is gone. They will not believe that and will assume you are just selfishly hoarding all your food now for yourself. They will band together into a mob to take your food by force and if you or your family dies in the process that will just be too bad for you. Or best case scenario is they just take all of your remaining food and leave you and your family healthy enough to beg for food just like them.

Or maybe you are heavily armed and when you realize that you must save the remainder of your food for your own family and you will kill to protect the small amount of food that you have left. So now you likely will have to shoot and kill all those same beggars that you have been feeding. At that point how have you helped them by feeding them? How have you helped your own family by drastically reducing the amount of stored food you have in storage?

The most logical answer is to turn away all the beggars in the first place, but again this is a personal decision you will likely have to make. Americans are overall a giving people. It goes against the grain to turn away those in need. In the above situation where a disaster is long term, you will have to live with whatever decision you choose to make. The best time to think about it is now instead of then.

One answer is to give your extra food to the local food shelf or church, in times of need. Let them disperse the food to those in need, and the needy do not have to know the food originally came from you. This way you and your family are safer without anyone knowing that you have stored food, but still you are helping your fellow man.

Like I said it is a very personal decision. I might have made you think I am against giving to those in need but that was not my intention. I was merely showing you a possible poor outcome if you did choose to share your food. Again it is a personal choice to make, and obviously, circumstance would change what decision you would make. But while making preparations for your family also keep your friends and neighbors in mind. Either get additional food to give away or plan on turning them away and not giving away any of your stored food.

And that is one of the reasons that ANY preparations you choose to make for the future safety of your family should be a secret. Everyone who knows that you are ready for any emergency will promptly make their way to your house as soon as the electric power goes off or it starts to rain or snow or any other possible disaster situation occurs.

They will demand to borrow your generator. They will demand to borrow some fuel for their generator. They will demand to borrow your gas grill and propane. They will demand that you feed them. Refuse, and things could easily get very ugly quickly.

If no one knows what you have, then it can be your choice if you decide to share something or not. Some old sayings are very true like 'Loose lips sink ships.' If no one knows that you have stuff it will be *your* choice if you share. If everyone knows you have stuff, it will more likely be *their* choice if you share.

Look at how many people act at stores having a Black Friday sale; they get aggressive, pushing and shoving and often even fighting. If they do that now over saving a few bucks on something that they likely don't even need, just think how they will act when they are starving and 'think' you have food?

Planning on hunting for food? Well so is everyone else. And the sound of a shot can be heard for a very long ways. This can draw the guy that does not know how to hunt but does know how to shoot so he can take that deer you carefully stalked and killed. Also, there will likely be roving packs of feral dogs, and they will soon associate that the sound of a gunshot means food for them. A gut pile from a dead deer or a dead hunter someone else shot or you if you are busy gutting out your fresh kill, it will be both the dead deer and you on the dog's menu. The dogs will get food from any of those scenarios.

Caution will be needed all the time. Many people will be trying to hunt for food, and even a poor hunter is lucky sometimes. Wild game numbers in easily accessible areas will diminish rapidly until only the smartest and fastest animals are left alive. But that is for easy assessable areas. If you live in the boon docks far from any urban center then wild game will not diminish in numbers so quickly. Same with fish in the rivers and lakes though that will likely take much longer to have greatly reduced numbers. So sure, supplement your stored food with fresh wild supplies when you can but only depend on what you have stored, the wild stuff, whether plant or animal, will only be a possibility, not a sure thing.

Snares and traps will be very useful for an easy and quiet way to add fresh meat. Both are indiscriminate so they might get you a fat rabbit or a skunk or a cat or the neighbor kid. The snare you set in the deer trail could just as easily kill a kid running down the trail. As with everything use with caution and try to think ahead. Also if someone sees you set snares or traps, they can make it a point to check them daily before you. Or just take them and set them elsewhere.

Garden seeds should be included in your preparations if you do not live in an apartment so in theory, you can then grow at least some of your own food in desperate times. Garden seeds are very inexpensive and take up little storage space. And most things you grow you can harvest the seeds from so you have some to plant the next year again. At a dollar store you can often buy four packages of seeds for a dollar.

Growing a large garden takes a lot of work, a lot of water, and some amount of knowledge or skill. Once you try growing your own food, you will no longer call them 'dumb farmers' ever again. Obviously, some things will be easier to grow than others and some things you likely will not like to eat. If the only thing out of a garden that you would consider eating is some watermelon, then don't bother buying any turnip seeds.

Some things like potatoes you grow from the potato itself. You cut them up, and you can get three or four or more new plants from just one potato. A single potato plant may produce a dozen large tasty potatoes.

A garden can be any size from one square foot to a hundred acres. You can even have a hanging garden to save space! You can grow many things in pots. Many people now often grow some spices or herbs in their homes in simple flower pots to have a fresh supply. Growing things inside your house or apartment in pots keeps it safe from animals and from raiding by pesky humans.

In most cases, your garden will have to be watered, so you have to plan for that when you figure out your water supply. If you have to get your water out of a lake that is a half mile away, your garden is just not going to work out very well for you.

In town, you will have to keep other people from picking the stuff in your garden. In the country, you will have to keep every critter out of your garden. You will likely learn to pray for rain and to pray for no hail. The neighbor's cow or pig could get out and totally destroy your whole garden before you get a single thing out of it. A garden is a great prep item but remember that it is not a sure thing because many things can cause a garden to fail.

Some now recommend planting a guerrilla garden. This is planting seeds at different spots in the general area and leaving them on their own, and you only check them when it's picking time. This has many benefits, like no maintenance, in several spots, so some are likely to survive (all your eggs are not in one basket), concealed from other humans, and does not disrupt having a regular garden at your home. Downsides are because of no maintenance it likely means very poor results, other humans might find it and reap the benefits, wild animals might eat everything, and you did remember all the spots where you planted them right?

Here again, if you have never done any gardening and are planning on it for your very survival at least get a book or two to read first. And remember you can try many different things in pots inside or outside your house first. Plant a potato in that big patio flower pot to try your hand at gardening. There are often some instructions printed on the backs of seed packets to at least get you started correctly.

So let's look at options for your survival food. First and most reliable is your stored food. Second is food out of your garden, a good choice but not a for sure source of food. The third is being a hunter/gatherer and living off the land. This is certainly not a sure source of food and could be dangerous but might work at least short-term or as an add-on. Fourth is to scavenge/steal/beg/barter food from others, this might be viable but dangerous and not for sure and maybe not very ethical or practical.

If you have pets or livestock are you going to store food for them also? Or is your plan to use your pets *AS* food? Either would be an acceptable answer. In a long-term situation, pets and livestock will be a valuable source of protein. Many say they will share their people food with their pets and this may be perfectly fine in short-term situations.

In long-term scenarios, you should have stored pet food, and when that runs out, your pet can become a food source for your real family. Does your pet really mean more to you than your son or daughter? If your choice is not to eat your pet then you should humanely dispatch the creature when your stored pet food is gone and if possible donate that meat to a neighbor so the valuable meat resource does not go to waste.

Under no circumstances should you ever just put your pet out to fend for itself. That pet is totally your responsibility, not anyone else's. Pets that are 'turned loose' often die a horrible slow death by starvation or the lucky ones are killed and eaten by other animals (or humans).

Even if living in the suburbs you can maybe grow some livestock right now. You could raise chickens for meat and/or eggs. You don't need a rooster to get eggs, and the rooster is the only loud one. You can also raise rabbits. They are obviously quiet and do not require very much room. Remember for any pet or livestock you also have to plan on their water supply also.

I have had to carry water to livestock on occasion and I can tell for a fact that water is heavy. If the power ever goes out and your water source is even fifty yards from your livestock, add a cart or other means to your preps to assist in moving the water rather than just carrying it.

Calories. If you are carrying water much distance you will be burning through many calories. If you are walking many miles out hunting you will be burning calories. Plan your food supply to your expected needs. If you will be inside your house hunkered down all day, every day then you will not need to consume as many calories per day. You could live on maybe fifteen hundred calories. If you will be getting plenty of exercise then you might need two times that many calories and possibly even more than that each day.

Many people buy pre-packaged long term storage foods in package deals. It might be a single bucket that is supposed to feed one person for a week or several buckets that are supposed to feed a family for a year. These are simple and easy to buy and store but likely are not a best choice. In many cases it will include food that your or some of your family will not want to eat or cannot eat because of food allergies. Also the calorie count on these package deals is often lacking. A serving might only be a hundred calories and a whole day's amount might be well less than a thousand calories. Way too few calories to survive on without losing body weight and muscle mass. A good rule of thumb is to cut the supposed time in half, if it says enough for one year then assume it is only enough for six months instead.

No matter how much food I would have stored if I thought a long-term situation was at hand, I would buy as much more food as I could just before the event if I had any advance notice. After water, food is the next most vital thing that you need in a long-term situation, and you will need way more food than you think. A common rule is five hundred pounds of food per person per year.

It is difficult to stress the importance of having stored food. And don't forget things like spices, bullion, BBQ sauce, ketchup, salad dressing, salsa, salt (and add more salt because it has many uses), peanut butter, jelly, sugar, brown sugar, and many more add-on items (like a spare can opener). These are easy to forget, and while we can likely get by without most of them, they will certainly enhance our dining experiences while using up little extra space or much more money spent.

Often longer term storage food (or wild food) can be a little bland, but with a few of these things added, a good cook can make any of us want to eat it. As a forager, I can tell you from experience that while many wild plants are certainly edible, in most cases, the application of your favorite salad dressing makes them much more edible.

An often missed large source of food

If you live in farming country, then you have very likely seen grain bins. Huge grain bins store an unbelievable amount of very edible grain. These bins are found near highways for ease of trucking or near railroad tracks for the same reason of shipping. Grain elevators store large amounts also, and those are common in towns and cities. Corn, oats, soybeans, and wheat are the common grains found in those bins. In most cases to use the grain best, you would need a grain mill. Or you could rub the grain between two rocks to make meal or flour. Or sprout the grain and eat the resulting sprouts.

When food is gone farmers will still very likely have grain still stored in those bins on their farms and that grain could be purchased or bartered for from those farmers. In desperate times grain bins in remote locations could be opened and grain removed for personal use. This would obviously be stealing, but that would be a choice every person would have to make if they and their family were starving.

Opening a door or chute near the bottom of a full grain bin can be very dangerous and cause a very considerable amount of waste. The grain will flow out just like opening a hole in a dam that is holding back water. It can quickly flow over you and cause suffocation. Be very careful if you ever need to access this source of food. Accessing from the top is always safest but do not fall in or you could basically drown in grain just like it was water.

Sundry Items

These are non-food items we often don't think much about. Things that we buy only occasionally and often are quite inexpensive. Things like toothbrushes and toothpaste, hand soap, dish soap, shampoo, laundry soap, toilet paper, feminine items, aspirin, contact lens cleaner, Band-Aids, and more little things that we use and need and should stock up on along with the food. Some people prep a large supply of these items with the plan of using them for barter during bad times. These items may be quite cheap now but would have real value in a long-term situation.

The list of these sundry items is almost endless. We all use and depend on so many little things that we think nothing about now, but we would sorely miss them if we had to do without. Most of these items we automatically toss in our shopping carts without a second thought. Would life be harder for you if you had no more of those reading glasses? Add some to your preps. Make a list of all the little things and add to that list as you think of more. When writing this list, you can add pencils and paper to the list, so you have them to write the next list.

Long-term items to stock might also include a pressure canner along with canning jars and canning lids. If your long-term plan includes using food from a garden, you will need many canning jars and a whole lot of lids. If you have plans for being off grid and yet have a freezer available to use then remember to stock some freezer paper to wrap your meat along with the tape for it.

Salt is a valuable storage item that is very inexpensive to purchase. Meat can be salted and dried for non-refrigerated storage. Making jerky also requires salt. Salt adds flavor to almost all foods.

A food dehydrator can either be an electric one that you buy or a passive solar one that you build or buy. A dehydrator can allow you to store many foods without refrigeration. Dehydrated foods are also much lighter to carry if you do any on-foot traveling. Remember little things like zip lock bags in different sizes as we all know they have hundreds of uses and can be easily forgotten when prepping.

If you have never baked bread (and this means most people), then it is something to try now. After going without bread for a time, a loaf of home baked bread is a real treat. And yes home baked is often way better than the stuff you buy. Eating a piece of bread fresh and warm from the oven is an experience everyone should enjoy, both now and after a disaster.

If you own your own home, you could maybe plant fruit and/or nut trees now. They often take several years before they produce but can be a real asset to your food storage plan and require very little maintenance.

Also, have plans to cook your stored or acquired food. You will need pans and a way to heat the food. If you plan on a camp stove of some kind make sure you have extra fuel for it. Same if you plan on using your grill, either gas or charcoal. Store wood of you plan on using a wood fire for cooking. And for sure have several ways to light the fire. Cigarette lighters, matches, scratch igniters, a magnifying glass, or other choices to start a fire. Or all of those choices.

You cannot get around it; storing extra food costs money. But unlike some prep items, single food items are quite low priced, and so even on a very small budget, you can slowly but steadily add to your food stores. Even budgeting five dollars a week or month toward extra food will soon show results. The key to doing it with less money is to use coupons and only buy prep foods when they are on sale. And remember- only buy what you will eat!

4. Shelter

The best shelter is likely your house or apartment. This is where you are the most comfortable. And you will likely still be comfortable there in an emergency situation if you make some preparations before the event. But no matter how much you prepare or where you live you should always have a backup plan in case you have to leave.

Many things can force you to leave your place of residence. A tornado can happen most places, and that can wreck any building. A fire can force you out. Or a chemical spill nearby, hurricane, snow/ice could collapse your roof, earthquake, sinkhole, volcano, overrun by bandits, plane crash on your dwelling; the list is almost endless. So while the best place to stay is likely where you now are you should definitely have a bug out plan or plan B just in case.

Supplies on hand will make any stay during an emergency more pleasant. Store water and food then just stay in your home as a shelter that covers the three big things for survival. You can always have more 'stuff' at your home than anywhere else. One of the big things we prep for is short or long-term loss of electric power. Most of us have already encountered loss of electric power for different reasons and different lengths of time.

While maybe not too practical for real long-term use a generator is great for short term outages. Generators come in many sizes and price ranges. From $100 or less for a small one from Harbor Freight to a large permanent automatic one that could cost thousands. And each of us has different needs so it is difficult to say which size you personally should get if any.

The first thing you should know when thinking about electrical is that anything used to produce heat draws a lot of power. Examples are a toaster, heater, coffee pot, hairdryer, microwave, or hot plate. These items draw maybe 1000 to 1500 watts each. An average homeowner size generator might be 3000 to 5000 watts. So you could, in theory, use two or three of these items at once.

A refrigerator might draw 400 or 500 watts. A central air conditioner might draw 5000 watts or more. A well pump might draw 3000 to 5000 watts. With a generator, you have to pick out the things that YOU think are important to you and what you might want to have on at the same time and then size the generator accordingly. A watt is a watt, and every electric item has a little plate or tag that lists how much it draws for electric power.

This can get a little complicated because sometimes it is listed in watts and then it is easy. Sometimes it is listed in amps like "3.2amp at 120 volt". In this case, you multiply the amps times the volts, so 3.2 times 120 equals 384 watts. Also, anything with a motor draws way more when it starts than when it is running, like ten times as much or more for a very short time. So that refrigerator that runs on 400 watts might draw two or three thousand watts when it starts up. This big load would only be for a couple of seconds or so but still must be allowed for in your planning.

You can look at items you want to operate and read the amount of electric draw, write it down and go to the store selling the generators and they can help you size the generator to fit your needs. Then you will have to plug the items directly into the generator or have a 'transfer switch' installed to direct the flow of generator power to the spots where you want it.

Another option is solar power or a 'solar generator.' Many places sell a 'solar generator,' but these can usually be built yourself for ½ or even ¼ of the cost of the advertised one. You can easily do a search online to buy or build your own. But either way, these always have very, very low capacity (no matter what the ad sounds like). These are for running lights or charging your phone/laptop or maybe at the very most running a small compact refrigerator. That is it, no microwave, no coffee pot, no heater type items on a solar generator.

There is one more way to get some temporary electrical power that is fairly inexpensive. Buy a power inverter that changes 12 volts (your car) to 120 volts like you have in your house. These inverters come in many different sizes and cost maybe $10 to $100 for a practical size to run from your car battery. The inverter would run small things like the 'solar generator' does (they use an inverter also). It is like a generator that is cheap because it uses your car motor (you have to have the car running, so you are using gas). Your car would work for some items on a short-term basis.

Or forget the electric power and go retro. Buy some candles and oil lamps for light. And yes oil lamps are readily available and throw way more light than a candle. Lamp oil will store a very long time. Cook with propane or wood or use a solar oven that you can buy or make yourself. A camp stove in either propane or white gas makes cooking hardly any different than if there was no catastrophe going on outside (as long as you also have the fuel on hand for that camp stove).

An easy option for some people is to buy an RV, and then you can have many comforts even when the power goes off. A motor home or a camp trailer or even a tent trailer as many benefits. One big benefit is if you have to bug out and leave your home you can still be quite comfortable. Used RV's can often be purchased very reasonably.

The biggest downside to owning an RV is where to keep the thing after you buy it. A typical RV has a propane powered refrigerator/freezer, a propane oven and cooktop, possibly hot and cold running water, maybe a bathroom, and comfy beds. Often has its own generator for the microwave and other electric items. For leaving your home, an RV can work well and even staying at home, you might find living in the RV easier if there is no power in your home.

Bugging out with no RV? Then a tent takes up very little storage space and is fairly reasonable, and a used one can be found very cheaply. Bugging out and leaving your home will require you to bring many things with to make you somewhat comfortable. This will mean a car or even a pickup with a trailer, depending on how much you want to take with you and how comfortable you want to be.

When you get a tent try hard to get one that is not brightly colored. Get one in an earth tone color. There is no advantage to a bright color, but there could very well be an advantage to a drab color. Always be thinking drab and thinking concealment with everything you do or buy. Your outer clothing should be in earth tones also. Same with your backpack. If you ever need to be concealed, then you will be thankful for those drab colors.

Whether in a car or an RV, if you are bugging out wear your hiking clothes and strong hiking shoes or boots when you are in the vehicle. Have a backpack packed and handy, so if something happens, you can grab your backpack and bail out of the vehicle. Certainly, odds are you will not have to, of course, but always think about being prepared for the unexpected, always.

What should you have in your pack? I don't like lists, and everyone would logically carry different things because of their own particular set of circumstances. Is it winter or summer? Are you alone or with others? Are you in the wet southeast, the dry southwest, the wide-open prairie, by the ocean, wooded area, in a heavily settled area, or in the middle of nowhere?

Some things are always good to have- a tarp, at least two ways to make a fire, a good strong knife, a map of the area, two compasses, some food, some water with a way to purify more, some cordage, extra socks and maybe other clothes. Whenever you carry things, it is always a trade-off; weight and bulk versus need.

Obviously, the best bet is to stay with your vehicle if possible. You can carry a lot of stuff in your vehicle, and the vehicle itself can always be your shelter. You might have to leave your vehicle to be closer to a water supply or for a different reason. Once you are bugging out and away from your residence, you might have to be much more flexible in your thinking. Like your shelter can be anything. If it is hot, maybe all you need is some shade. Your particular situation and location make all the difference.

While staying in your home is often the best choice (especially short-term) in some cases that is just not the best case. If you are in an apartment or a condo they can become poor places to stay very quickly in many situations. Both are very susceptible to fire. With either, you have many other people staying in the same building, and if any of them start a fire, all must evacuate very quickly. Also, those buildings are often located near the center of the city or town and could be very close to any 'social unrest' or riots. Often it is quite difficult to be very secure in those buildings.

Another problem with any living quarters in a city or town is if the power goes off you lose your water supply. You can prepare for this somewhat by storing some water, but lack of power also means lack of sewage pumps. This could cause raw sewage to back up into your house or apartment. As you can imagine this could force your evacuation. Living on the second floor or higher or living on a hill will help prevent sewage backup from entering your home or apartment. Too bad for the people on the first floor because they will know every time someone above flushes.

Evacuating from a city or town could be problematic depending on many factors. If many people are trying to leave at the same time, the roads will likely be clogged possibly to the point of no movement. Earthquakes, or fires, or other natural disasters can close off certain roads or even large sections of the town or city. Plot several routes that you can use to leave the area and try them out to find their weak or strong points, and so you get familiar with the routes. If at all possible have plans to evacuate in more than one direction in case one route gets completely out of the question.

Plan in case you are unable to evacuate with your vehicle. A bike could be used, or you can always walk. If you own a motorcycle, they can often be ridden where cars cannot go because of tight spaces that might be encountered. To carry more stuff on a bike or motorcycle, you can install panniers (saddlebags) or attach a small trailer. Walking means a backpack or some kind of a cart or even a wheeled suitcase.

Any weight that can be put on wheels instead of on your back will make it a lot easier to bug out (more stuff with less fatigue). Detailed maps can be invaluable to have, and you should have the actual paper printed form and not just depend on your GPS or smartphone. Have real paper detailed maps of your area. If you think you might at some point try to evacuate on foot, try it beforehand. Just leave your house or apartment and walk your planned evac route. Don't even carry a pack the on the first try. Just try it and when you get tired you can call a cab to get back home again. That will give you a good idea of your capability of on-foot evacuation.

Do you have any pets? What is your plan for your pets if you have to evacuate? Evacuating with your pets would likely be fine if you can use your vehicle but what if you have to leave on foot? A medium-sized or larger dog can be put on a leash and be taken with you without causing a lot of trouble but are you going to put a leash on each of your three cats? Can you carry all of them at once?

Are you going to carry food and water for your pets? Many people have more than one dog. Can you walk them on a leash together? What if you have a cat or two? It would not be practical to carry a cat or try to walk it on a leash. So what is your plan? Let the cat loose to become some else's problem? Turn it loose to die a slow death from starvation? Leave them trapped in your dwelling with extra food and water? I do not have an answer for what you should do with your pets if you ever have to evacuate your home quickly but I do know that the time to think of your plan for pets is well before something happens.

Alternate shelter

It is a good idea to have an alternate shelter lined up if you ever need it. Or several choices are even better. Alternates can be a friend's house or apartment or the home/apartment of a relative or even a motel. Maybe it is a favorite camping spot you have camped at before that is not too far away. Maybe it is your RV, and it can be driven or pulled most anywhere. Or maybe you have a cabin or second home.

Many call this alternate place their BOL for bug out location. Your alternate should be at least some distance from your normal living quarters. A friend's apartment in the same building might be handy but would do no good if the building is on fire. A friend a few blocks away might be fine but across town or in the country nearby might be a better choice. That is why a couple of possible locations would give you much more flexibility.

An alternate location within ten miles could be reached by foot in less than a day for many people. Try not to have your main BOL more than a half a tank of gas away from your regular home. So maybe we are talking within two hundred miles maximum from your home with several possible routes to get there and possibly friendly stops setup along the route, like a friend's house.

If possible, it would be a good idea to stash at least a few things at this other location just in case you show up there with nothing but the clothes on your back. Handy things to stash there might be some clothes (include shoes!), maybe some cash, spare cell phone charger, special medications that you need, backpack/camping gear, or whatever you think might make your stay there easier and safer or to use to re-supply you to continue your journey to a different destination. Maybe some stabilized fuel if it is more of a re-supply depot on the route to your BOL. This is possible if this spot is a friend/relative's house. If this spot is just a camping spot then stashing supplies there would not be practical or at least it could be problematic. This re-supply spot could also be a rental storage place but that would also mean a monthly fee you would have to pay.

Explore alternate routes to get to this BOL. Do this until you are familiar enough with each of these other routes, so you do not need a map (but have a paper map with – always). In an emergency situation of just about any kind, you can expect roads to be closed off or clogged with cars. That is why you plan ahead for these different routes.

Even plan a route or two for if you are on foot or on a bike. Do you have to cross a river or stream? What if the bridge is down or completely blocked? Earthquakes can happen almost anywhere even though you might not have heard of one happening near you in the past. That could cause many different routes to be impassable and that is why you need alternates. But many things can cause a route to be closed down. A large accident might close even a major highway for many hours. Police might close down highways due to nearby wildfires. There can be many reasons for any road or even major highways to close so you must be ready to go a different way.

5. Security

Security is to be safe in both your body and your possessions. There is only one entity that is in charge of your security, and that is you. It is totally your responsibility. After knowledge, I feel security is the next most important prep you can do. What good is having prepared for everything if someone steals what you have acquired? Or worse yet you end up dead at the hands of another human.

Even if there is never a disaster this prep is very worthwhile (and may be life-saving). If you own a home, you can do much to increase your security but if you rent you can still do some but not as much. One common thing is to increase your personal security. There are a few things all of us can do to make us more secure when we are out and about.

The first thing is totally free and can be done by every single one of us, and it can greatly enhance our safety. But it is difficult because it requires effort and thinking on our part. It is to be aware of our surroundings at all times.

We are all so wrapped up in our personal lives and our own trials and tribulations that we don't ever really look at our surroundings. You do not have to be on your phone in public, whether it is talking on the phone or surfing the internet with it or texting. Stay off your phone in public. When you are talking, you are always giving away personal details about your life to everyone within earshot. Plus you are totally distracted from your surroundings when you are on the phone.

The next step is to train yourself to look around. That seems simple enough, but almost no one does it. And that is why you have to train yourself to do it because you are conditioned not to right now. Keep your head up and look around and notice what you are seeing. If you can make yourself do this, you will be way safer than ninety percent of the people around you. Look at the people around you. I mean LOOK at them. Look at not just cars but the people in those cars. Look ahead of you and to the sides and occasionally to the rear. Even look up. It does not seem like a hard thing to do, but you will likely find that it is almost impossible. Just keep it in the back of your mind at all times.

The next thing you can do costs money but has multiple benefits. Take a martial arts class. A good class will teach you some self-defense and some self-confidence. You don't have to be a black belt, just learn a few simple self-defense moves.

To be good at martial arts or any fighting you have to be a good athlete which very few people are. That is why real athletes make so much money. It is because they are 'special.' God gave them that something, they did not learn it, they were born with it. But we all can learn some stuff that will help us survive.

And yes everyone can train and make themselves better at something like this but we all are not Chuck Norris and never will be. The martial arts class will teach you some self-defense, and it will help you get into better shape physically. It will also make you more flexible. There are at least three benefits; training, fitness, and flexibility, three things for the price of one. Oh, actually four things because you will be healthier too.

Maybe now is the time to talk about victims and a little about fear. There is nothing wrong with fear. We are designed to feel fear to help keep us safe. It is obviously a good thing to be fearful of jumping off a building because it would cause us harm. Fear is natural and not something to be ashamed of by any means.

Occasionally fear can harm us by causing inaction. Like when someone is 'frozen in fear.' Sometimes fear can cloud our minds from logical thinking. While fear is natural, you do want to be in control of it and not let the fear be in control of you.

Sometimes we can learn to face and overcome our fears (like fear of flying or fear of drowning). Being physically fit and being knowledgeable can give us confidence, and that helps us control our fear. Anyone and I do mean anyone, can freeze at an inopportune time whether you are a navy seal or a schoolteacher. All any of us can do is prepare the best we can. Exercise, a martial arts class, and knowledge all will help you gain confidence and be prepared for what comes your way. Earlier I talked about awareness. Being aware of your surroundings. This can not be stressed enough. Being aware is the best life-saving tool or ability that you can possess.

Don't want to be a victim? If faced with a situation that could likely lead to your death my advice (though it may be unpopular) is to fight. Do not give up but fight and keep fighting. Whether you are a man, woman or child, choose not to be a victim and fight.

If running is a viable option then by all means run but if running is pointless or impossible then fight. Don't be squeamish and don't try to be fair. Use your hands, your feet, your elbows, your teeth, or your head.

Remember just about anything can be a weapon; a rock, an ink pen, a coffee mug, a high heeled shoe, your keys, most anything; if it is harder than your hand then hit them or poke them with it. This is your life we are talking about so do not be nice or squeamish.

Poke or scratch their eyes out. Strike them in the throat, more than once if possible. Their nose is tender so hit it as hard as you can. If you have teeth, then use them and not in a playful way, bite and try to remove a chunk with your teeth. Kick them in the shin or the knee or the groin.

Got a solid heel on your shoe then bring it down on the top of their foot as hard as you can. Every act should be with as much power as you can manage. If they double over that just means their head is within easy reach of your foot. Kick them in the face or if possible in the throat.

If you get the upper hand, then keep up the attack until they are no longer a threat and make sure that they really are no longer a threat. If they hit the ground that does NOT mean they are no longer a threat to you because they can likely get up again and attack you or grab your legs and drag you to the ground.

Don't think you can do any of that? OK then you can just be a victim, and it is still possible that you will live through the encounter. The difference is that if you fight, then you have a vote in your survival but if you do not fight your attacker has total control, and you must abide with his decision whether you are to live or to die. Do you want your very life to be the sole decision of a bad guy?

In some areas, you can carry tools for defense but always remember that anything you have can be taken from you and used against you. What tools can you carry? That depends on local laws and where you will be. Most places of employment outlaw most tools of defense.

But you do still have options that can increase the chance of your survival. You can carry an ink pen about anywhere. It can be made out of plastic or be made out of metal. There are ones called 'tactical pens,' and a quick internet search will show you many different ones to choose from.

Most of us carry a key ring. One of those 'keys' can be ground down to more of a point, and anyone can do this. Take an unused key or have a spare key made then file or grind it or just rub the key on the cement until it has a sharper point. Ten minutes rubbing it on some cement while sitting in the park will give you a make-shift tool for defense. No need to make it like a needle just to a somewhat sharper point. Keys are often made out of a soft metal called brass and are easy to file or grind. This sharp key can be used as a weapon with some effect; again the eyes or throat are good targets for this defensive tool.

There are many different types of knives that can be hidden (some in plain sight!) but use caution as many are forbidden by local laws. There are expandable batons that with training become very formidable weapons. Or pepper spray or a stun gun. Again check local laws first. A cane or walking stick can always be carried everywhere and can be an excellent tool for defense. Only you need to know the reason you are using a cane.

And there are guns. Most states now allow concealed carry of guns for self-protection with a permit and a few states allow it without a permit. Permits can be easy or difficult to get, but most require taking a class before they are issued. Taking a class is certainly a good thing whether it is a requirement or not.

Carrying a gun is a big step and certainly not for everyone whether legal or not. Never carry a gun unless you would be willing to use it to take the life of another to save your own life. Never carry a gun unless you are proficient in its use. Know where you can and can not carry a gun. For instance, you cannot carry a gun into a federal building (like a post office). State laws vary about where you can carry and where you can not.

The steps for carrying a firearm would be something like this. First is the decision to carry with the knowledge that doing so may require you at some point to take the life of another person.

Second would be to thoroughly research the laws of carrying in your state and if you are eligible to do so. Third/fourth is to take a concealed carry class. Third/fourth is to pick out a gun that fits you well and meets your criteria for size, weight, power, price, comfort, or any other criteria you decide is important.

Fifth is to practice until you are proficient and very familiar with your gun. Then after receiving your permit, you can start to carry.

A good class will teach you the many bad things that carrying/using a gun could involve. There is only one good thing, and that is it may save your life (or possibly the life of another). While this is the only advantage to carrying a gun, it is obviously a pretty good one.

Some of the bad things are that you are at risk of having your gun taken and it then used against you and/or others. Or that if you justifiably kill or wound an attacker you will still likely be arrested (all are treated as a homicide) and first a prosecutor then maybe a jury will decide if you are innocent or should go to prison. The old saying "I would rather be judged by twelve than carried by six" is a true saying and something you should think about before deciding to carry a weapon. Keep in mind that most states view any weapon the same as a gun. A baton, a knife, or even stun gun, are all still considered a weapon just like a firearm.

Also, you can be arrested if you forget and carry in a prohibited location. In some states, you can face a fine or arrest if your concealed gun happens to become partially visible. If you like to occasionally have an alcoholic drink that is usually not an option while you carry.

Then there is the fact that you will be now lugging around a one to three-pound piece of mostly metal that is often uncomfortable and has an extremely small chance of ever being used. There is much to know and much responsibility if you decide to carry a gun. It is also the best defensive tool that you can carry and a true equalizer for the old or weak.

Home Security

So that is some about your personal security then there is your home security. If you live in an apartment, there are obviously fewer options that you can do to enhance your security. In almost all cases you can do no permanent changes to anything which severely limits your options. Anything that I happen to list for apartment dwellers can usually also be done by homeowners.

If you have an apartment, you have no idea who or how many people have keys to your apartment. The landlord has one, and you have no idea how many people he gives keys to. Things to do first are to remove the screws for the hinges and strike plates on your door and if those screws are short (often an inch or even less) replace them with longer screws and if possible increase the size (diameter) also. Your landlord does not need to know you have done this and the change will not be visible when done, and it does not hurt anything, it only makes everything stronger.

Next is a door security bar. This is just a metal bar that is designed to wedge under the doorknob and then angle down to the floor. Sometimes people have propped a chair under the doorknob to prevent the door from being opened but a tool made for that exact purpose, a door security bar is way better at this job. These cost maybe fifteen to twenty-five dollars and require no permanent installation while making your home or apartment much more secure and can be removed instantly in case of fire. They are not permanent, and some people use them when traveling while staying in motels (a great idea). This simple device that you can make yourself is likely the primary way you can make yourself more secure while you are in your residence and they can even be used on your bedroom door for a second level of nighttime security.

Sliding patio doors are often found in both homes and in apartments. These doors are anything but secure. The most common way to make them more secure is to lay a rod or a wood dowel (maybe a broom handle) in the track on the bottom to prevent the door from sliding in the track. Do this, it costs almost nothing, requires no installation, and definitely increases security.

A longer bar or rod can be placed at an angle from the top of the sliding door to the end of the track on the bottom. This can be done in conjunction with the bar lying in the track. Using both stops movement of the door on both the top and the bottom.

Sometimes a couple of holes can be drilled (if they are not already present) through the sliding door track on top and/or bottom and a simple pin (or a common nail) inserted to prevent the movement of the door. These things all make the patio door slightly more secure, but it is still a very weak link in your home security.

That is just the nature of these doors. They can often just be lifted up a little bit from the outside and removed from the track and just set aside. A pin or screw through the top track can prevent this (or at least make it harder). And obviously, the glass door can always be smashed open using whatever can be found near it.

Most windows have locks on them, and obviously, these should always be used. Methods used to secure sliding doors can also be used on sliding windows (pins and/or rods). The time to make your residence more secure is BEFORE something happens. The old saying 'Locking the barn after the horse is stolen' is so very true. Many people think about their home security only after their home has been broken into. At least they then think about it then if they are still alive.

I am not a big technology guy, but as long as we have the technology, then we should embrace it and use it for our advantage. Many people buy and use security cameras. When they are visible from the outside of your home, they can act somewhat as a deterrent for break-ins. They obviously do not stop anyone from entering.

Once someone is inside, they can find and destroy the recording device (if it is on site and they have the time). Even if you have the recorded images of the perpetrators stealing your stuff, it would have limited value.

Your stuff is still gone, and you are unlikely ever to see it again. It is always best to stop someone from entering your home rather than recording them after they are inside. If you have cameras outside and monitor them while you are home, then you can conceivably see bad guys approaching and can take action.

Motion sensor outdoor lights are a deterrent and can sometimes be installed even in a rental property. A dog can be a deterrent but ninety percent of the time they are not a very good deterrent but can still act as an alarm. But many dogs bark so often that they are soon dismissed when they bark (or only told to 'shut up').

For homeowners there are many things you can do to increase your security besides those listed above. Let's start at the doors. Doors can be replaced, and heavier solid core doors can be installed (often expensive!). Locks can be replaced with higher quality and stronger models.

If your lock comes from a hardware store or Home Depot, it is not a very secure lock. Better locks start at about one hundred and fifty dollars each. Cheaper locks can be easily opened with bump keys or can be easily picked, or other methods can be used to open them. There is a reason that some locks cost fifteen dollars and some cost one hundred and fifty dollars.

Heavy-duty strike plates and lock re-enforcement plates can be installed. When done properly your door can no longer be opened with a simple kick and even the police with their heavy door bashers will have quite a time getting in.

Steel security doors can be installed with quality locks, and then you have two heavy layers of protection at the common entry points. The big advantage with a steel security door is you can then open your existing door and talk to someone outside and still be quite secure behind that steel locked security door.

Patio doors can be changed to French doors that offer slightly more security. Or steel security doors can be installed over the existing patio doors. Patio doors can have security film installed on them. It can not be seen but makes the glass harder to break and the glass hangs together if it does break making entry tougher.

Windows alone and windows in doors can have security film installed that makes them much harder to break and keeps the window together if it is broken. This is a great invisible security enhancement.

Steel security shutters can be installed that can be operated manually or at the push of a button. Window coverings like curtains or drapes can be used to prevent people from seeing into your home and exposing all your secrets.

Metal, tile, or slate can be used for roofing to make your home more secure from fire. Stucco, brick, rock, or metal siding can be installed for fire resistance also.

You can make sections of your home highly bullet resistant with some lumber and sand. Buy some two by six lumber and some half inch plywood. Make some simple boxes that are six inches thick and fill them with dry sand or crushed rock. These boxes can then be attached to your house and finished like the rest of your house with siding, stucco, rock face, or just painted to match the rest of your house. Those six inches of rock or sand will stop most bullets and can be done only four feet high to give you quite a bit of protection from gunfire. If done right it will just look like an architectural element of the home, and only you will know its true function as bullet-resistant protection. As a side benefit the mass of sand will help keep the inside temps in your home more even.

Welded steel wire fencing comes in many sizes and styles. Something with one inch by one inch or one inch by two-inch mesh openings can be put over windows to keep rocks or Molotov cocktails from being thrown through them. It will also likely stop tear gas from being thrown or shot into the home by police.

These can be made up ahead of time to the exact size of your windows using angle iron or two by two lumber and installed when you think the time is right. These would also stop a lot of windblown debris from breaking the windows during a hurricane and will deter bad guys from entering through the windows.

They can be painted to match the window frame and are hard to see without getting quite close to the home. If installed permanently keep in mind that they will prevent you from using the windows as an emergency exit very easily.

Perimeters of your land can be 'fenced' the old fashioned way with 'briars and brambles.' Many things like raspberry or blackberry bushes can help restrict ingress/egress and supply food also. Even rose bushes are very pretty but can make a good addition to a 'fence.' The rose petals and rose hips are also very edible. These natural fences are often a better deterrent than modern metal fences.

The simple fact is that most homes are very poor defensive positions. A rifle bullet from outside will likely pass through two or more rooms before stopping or even go through the whole house and exit the other side.

Usually, there is good cover and concealment outside the house that attackers can use. Often there are higher elevation positions for attackers to use against you. Most houses can be easily started on fire. Or a nearby building or trees can be started on fire to smoke out those holed up in the house.

Most houses have a very poor field of fire. Most houses have no kind of barrier to stop a vehicle from being crashed into the house. Most house doors can be opened with just a hard kick. Many houses have a total blind side that contains no windows.

The time to think about defending your home is way before that need ever arises. If you can plainly see that your home can not be much improved and will always be non-defensible then plan when and how you will evacuate and where you will go if the situation in your area ever gets really bad.

Sometimes a like-minded neighbor can mean that both houses are way better defended simply by working together. It is a simple fact that a single family cannot watch all four sides of their house twenty-four hours a day. Logically that would take four trained people at all times working eight-hour shifts which means twelve capable people in the home just for security working in shifts.

You can always start by walking around the physical structure of your home and making a note of any vulnerability from a security standpoint. Think how you would attack your own home. And think vicious because those who attack you will be vicious. Likely you don't need so many windows or as big of windows.

Think how you can easily and effectively close off some windows on a temporary basis. Maybe it means making strong shutters or having wood pre-cut and marked for which window that it is made to fit. If the windows are inset, you can make more of the sand-filled boxes that custom fit in those inset windows. This would make that window also bullet resistant. But do not close off any windows if that means there will be blind spots that you can not see from inside your home. Remove hiding spots that attackers can use around your home. You can also plant cactus or thorn bushes under windows to deter the bad guys.

If trouble looks imminent, but you have some time things like simple boards will nails pounded through can be placed on the ground with the nails up and covered with grass clippings or sprinkled with dirt to hide them. They Will slow up attackers.

Plywood can be cut and securely screwed to your doors to make them even stronger.

Strings or fine wires can be stretched around and empty cans attached to help make a simple perimeter alarm. Or just as simple, heavier trip wires to trip those running toward your house. If they trip and fall onto some of those nail boards, they will be slower getting up.

Plan a way to safely escape your home and a meeting point for family members if you do evacuate your home. The meeting point should be fairly close to your house but far enough away to be safe and out of sight of your home. The meeting point can just be a spot nearby or a building or even a neighbor's house.

A cache is a hidden supply depot for some survival gear for yourself and your family. It should be far enough away from your house so if your home is compromised in any way you can still be safe while you access your cache. You can have multiple caches or just one or none.

They can be buried (how will you dig it back up?), or just hidden, or just be some stuff stored at a nearby friend or relative's place or even at a storage facility in the area. A cache might contain clothes, camping gear, food, water, guns, ammunition, cash, medicine, or whatever you think you might want/need and have the space for.

A cache can be very small even just some cash hidden away somewhere. Do you even need a cache? That is for you to decide if or how it might fit into your personal survival plan.

Some people use storage facilities to keep prep items and bug out items. It is certainly an option and in some cases might be your only viable option. These facilities are often broken into so if you do decide to use one lock it up to the best of your ability to do so.

If your compartment has a hundred dollar lock on it and the next ones only have ten dollar locks chances are they will break into the easier ones first. One person said he covered his real items he was storing with cheap items he had gotten at yard sales, often from the 'free box.' So anyone breaking in would only see a worthless pile of items that were not even worth stealing while the real stuff was safely hidden underneath.

A rented spot in a storage facility could be emergency living quarters at least long enough for you to thoroughly assess your options for leaving the area and be a spot for you to re-supply before continuing your evacuation from the area.

They make heavy steel lockable boxes for construction sites in many sizes, and one or two of these might be an option to keep items more secure inside a storage facility. You could add full sandbags to the bottom of these boxes to make them too heavy to be moved easily or even buckets of fresh water that would serve double duty. They are designed to be locked securely and to be very hard to get into. Instead of sandbags in them if two are used they could be bolted together and then would be very hard to move also or possibly attached to the floor or walls of the building.

Firearms

Any talk about security logically would include firearms. In most areas of the United States, you can still keep at least some kind of firearm in your home for protection. You might go to jail if you ever were to use it, but at least you would be still alive.

Local and state laws vary quite a bit so you will have to investigate your local laws before acquiring any firearms. There are many different opinions on what someone should own for defense, and there are hundreds of different firearms to choose from. Anything you do buy you should become very familiar with.

For personal and home defense, the two common choices are a handgun and/or a shotgun. Personally, I am not a fan of shotguns and would say get a handgun, but many make a good argument in favor of a shotgun.

If you plan on ever getting a concealed carry permit, then the only choice for that would be a handgun. Commonly you then have two choices – either a revolver or a semi-automatic. Naturally, they both have their good points and bad points. Many people own both and may carry one or the other on occasion.

Before buying a handgun especially, you should look at and handle as many as possible. Sometimes shooting ranges allow you to rent guns to shoot there so you can even shoot different ones to see what fits you best.

As far as my personal recommendation as to which you should buy between a revolver and an auto, I have no opinion. It is a personal choice, and that is why you should handle several different ones to see what 'feels good' in your hands.

I will say that if you are somewhat weak in your hands and if you like a semi-automatic then make sure you can easily 'rack the slide' without undue effort BEFORE you purchase one. This is in no way a condemnation of automatics, just stating a simple fact. I have seen both men and women have trouble working the action on some auto pistols. That is obviously never a problem with a revolver. I own both and am comfortable carrying and shooting either a revolver or a semi-automatic handgun.

Once you own a firearm, become proficient in its use. And buy some ammunition to keep on hand for it. Any gun is about worthless without ammunition. And of course, other than cost there is little reason to only purchase one firearm as likely most firearm owners have more than one.

For home defense and for hunting many preppers recommend owning three or four firearms. Commonly a handgun, a shotgun, a centerfire rifle, and a rimfire rifle. Some say have two centerfire rifles both a semi-automatic rifle (like AR-15, Mini-14, SKS, AK47 type rifle) and a scoped rifle capable of longer range shooting.

Guns are an expensive prep item, so my advice is if you have none now start with a 22 caliber rifle. If finances permit my suggestion would be a Ruger Model 10/22 (around $250). Or if finances are really tight then there are new 22 rifles available for about one half of that cost.

These are cheap to shoot, have basically no recoil, and are a good learning tool. A 22 rifle is an excellent prep item also (my first choice of a prep firearm). The ammunition is relatively cheap, takes up very little space to store and is much lighter than any other caliber. A 22 rifle makes less noise than other guns. And they are usually smaller and lighter than other long guns making them easier to handle.

I often recommend Ruger brand firearms. They are made in the USA, and most are made to take abuse and keep working. There are also many other brands that are excellent choices.

If I were only to have two firearms they would be a centerfire handgun and a 22 rimfire rifle. Many would argue for other choices, and that is fine as we all can have an opinion. With the money that firearms cost, do plenty of research and handle many different ones before you dish out the cash for several firearms and the ammunition to go with them.

Talk to twenty different gun owners, and you will get twenty different opinions on what you should buy. The fact is they could all be correct even though they are all different in their opinions. As we all have different experiences and are in different circumstances.

Briefly, a shotgun was originally designed to shoot at close range targets that are flying using ammunition that contains tens or even hundreds of small round lead balls. Ducks, geese, grouse or whatever that is flying and edible. That was their primary purpose.

Naturally, times have changed. Now many shotguns are designed just for defense. Some are designed to shoot accurately a single projectile out to maybe one hundred and fifty yards.

Ammunition for a shotgun is the bulkiest and heaviest of any ammunition making carrying much ammo a problem. Shotguns also have relatively small magazine capacity for that very same reason.

Rifles were designed for maximum power and range. Most still generally follow that design. Rifles can be purchased that have an effective range of a mile in the hands of an expert. Most centerfire caliber ammunition can actually travel for two or three times that distance.

Rifles can weigh anywhere from maybe two or three pounds up to thirty some pounds. Magazine capacity can be one round to over one hundred.

Other than target shooting most rifles are designed for shooting people or animals at a distance. Rifles are the most accurate of all guns. For a prepper, a rifle would be used for hunting small or big game of any size. Defense or offense would be another use.

Handguns were originally designed as an easily portable weapon for defense at close range. Most handguns still fall into this design role. Currently, most handguns for this role are a semi-automatic design that hold a magazine containing a number of rounds of ammunition and can fire a single round with each pull of the trigger.

The other common handgun fulfilling this role is a revolver. This type has a revolving cylinder containing five to ten shots.

Most are either five or six shot. Hence the old common name of 'six-shooter'.

There are many specialty handguns of many different designs and styles used for many purposes. For a prepper, a handgun could be valuable as a defensive weapon that could be easily concealed. Or as a hunting tool for either small, or even in some cases, big game.

There are hundreds of different model guns available. Most have good points and bad points. I could give you a list of likely possibilities to choose from, but really if you want a firearm, you should go looking yourself. Any suggestion I or anyone else give is always just an opinion. Without knowing your situation or what you want the gun for it is about impossible to make any kind of practical suggestion.

Visit a few gun shops. Ask questions and handle a few guns. Most people that handle guns for the first time are very surprised at how heavy they are in real life. So, by all means, handle several before buying any and get different opinions first from several different sources before buying one.

Believe me you would not be the first person to ever ask for advice on guns from a gun dealer. They are used to it and most are happy to make suggestions for you. Often the guy (or gal) behind the counter is quite knowledgeable and will be happy to give you the benefit of that knowledge. But they will give you mostly an opinion. And others might give you a different opinion. Ultimately you will have to decide what you like best and best fits your particular needs.

Other weapons

There are other weapons that could be useful to a prepper. A bow immediately comes to mind. These are quiet, and both the bow and the arrows can be made at home. Here again, they are now made in many different styles and configurations.

Bows and crossbows require some physical strength to use them. They are made in many different pull weights. These weapons also require practice to become proficient in their use. A bow and some arrows could likely be a useful addition to a prepper's supplies.

Another weapon that might be useful to a prepper is an air rifle. These are commonly somewhat quieter than a firearm and still, have the power to take small game at reasonable ranges.

A slingshot can still be used for taking small game as they have for many years.

6. The Value of Knowledge

No matter how much you prep and how much stuff you have there is always the risk of losing it all. From a natural event or from bandits you could lose everything. The one thing you can never lose is your knowledge. Read, read, read and whenever possible try the things that you have read about. Watch others that have skills and learn from them.

Often you can take simple community education classes for free or a small cost. Knowledge is power and could save your life or the lives of loved ones. First-aid classes are just one example. Knowledge can be found in many places. A neighbor, a friend, or a relative all might have a skill or knowledge that you can learn.

Go to a mountain man rendezvous, a civil war re-enactment, a thrashing show, the list is almost endless. Not a hunter? Take a state-approved hunter education class whether you plan to hunt or not as they are often full of valuable information at a very small cost.

A home and garden show or free seminar at a nursery can give knowledge about gardening. LDS churches sometimes teach about canning and other food storage ideas.

Look in the local paper for the event calendar. Many events give free or low-cost seminars on many different topics. Community colleges often have short classes on many subjects. State DNR or Fish and Wildlife departments often have free shooting or fishing events for beginners and this information could be extremely valuable. Some towns have 'community education classes' that are taught by local citizens on many topics at little or no cost.

Craigslist has events and classes listed in your area. That is just another spot to check.

Grandma and Grandpa know a lot of stuff and wanted you to visit them anyway. Go to them and talk and learn. They might not even realize just how valuable their store of knowledge is, but really it could literally save your life at some point in the future.

Don't limit your topics; open your mind to everything. You might easily find something that you thought you would have no interest in and instead find that you really enjoy it. I'm a guy, but when I was young, I had my mother teach me how to sew, and I have used that knowledge countless times since then.

Learn to cook over an open fire. Maybe first learn to make a fire. A campfire and a cooking fire are not necessarily the same. Often a very small fire not much bigger than your hand is all that is needed to cook your meal. You don't always need a fire big enough to be seen from space. Learn to just plain cook if you don't know how right now. Your mommy might not always be there to feed you.

Watch youtube videos. I think there is a youtube video on every subject ever known to man. Watch the videos then try the things yourself. The videos are a great teaching tool. And for free. Some are just funny, but many have actual great knowledge that someone you don't even know is trying to teach you and for free.

Your local library has thousands of books, and you can often order books that they don't have on hand. And did I mention it's free? If you are reading this, you likely have a Kindle or a free Kindle app (now this book is also in print) so look at all the free books Amazon offers and those free offers change daily (amazon.com/kindle-store).

Go to freereadfeed.com to see free Kindle books (every book they list is free). For the amount of space on your hard drive that one video game takes up you can store hundreds of Kindle books. Which is great but the best place to store knowledge is in your head. And remember if you actually do something once it is much easier to remember than if you just read about it.

Yard sales often have many books that can be bought cheap (along with a host of other useful items). Yard sales very often have how-to books that can give you a lot of knowledge. Haggling the price at a yard sale is common, and often the more you buy, the lower the price. Don't be shy; the dollar you save can then buy you another can of vegetables at the grocery store that you can add to your preps. Plus haggling itself is a skill that should be learned. Thrift stores sell tons of books and often have sales on a regular basis so you can get them even cheaper (while there look for other items of use too).

See if there is a hiking club in your area. Joining a hiking club has many benefits. It will help get you in better physical shape. When hiking with a group, you can learn local plants, animals, and trees. You can learn how to mark and/or stay on a trail. You can learn how to read maps and use a compass. You can learn your limits in case you ever think about bugging out on foot. You might find new friends that share your interests.

And actually **DO** stuff after you learn how. That is the best way to retain the knowledge, and then you know that you can really do it. Surprise your wife or husband with your new found skills. They will be impressed and proud of you.

Are you the only one in your household that will have any knowledge? Obviously not as everyone knows some stuff but try to get everyone in the household involved with learning valuable things. They all don't have to learn the same stuff, and it would be better if everyone learned different things anyway so your household would contain a broader range of knowledge.

Kids can be taught many things, and they are often eager to learn. Everyone should know how to start a cooking fire and how to keep it very small and the reason to keep it small. A bigger fire produces more smoke that will advertise your presence and the fact that you are cooking. A larger fire will use up way more of your fuel. A large fire is harder to contain and easy to 'get away' from you to become a wildfire. At night a big fire can be seen from quite a long distance whether that fact is good if you want to be rescued or bad if you are being hunted.

Everyone can learn some simple cooking. Everyone can learn what to pack in an emergency. Everyone can and should learn firearm safety (even if you decide Not to own any firearms). Everyone can learn how to safely load every firearm you own and how to fire it in case of an emergency.

Everyone at home can get into better shape physically. Everyone should be aware of and think about their personal security and the security of the home. Everyone should know how to sharpen a knife. How to light an oil lamp. Where everything is stored. How to start the generator and fill it with fuel. The survival of a family is the responsibility of the whole family not just one of them.

Some knowledge can be bought and stored in books. And I mean paper books, not just electronic books. Buy books and read them and then you can always go back and refresh your memory when you actually need to use that information.

Remember that you can always lose everything you own, but you cannot lose the knowledge that is stored in your head.

7. Ramblings

This section is for just short unrelated tidbits of information. It will only be a line or two then jump to something entirely different.

Almost all preparations are for relatively short-term survival; whether you have three days of food stored or a year's supply, it will run out at some point. Some folks strive for sustainability and self-sufficiency. An example would be an off-grid farm where some livestock and a large garden would produce enough food for the inhabitants year after year with maybe some excess to use for trading/bartering.

Some folks plan on using their skills for bartering for goods in a long-term survival event. Depending on the situation and location skills like a doctor, dentist, blacksmith, mechanic, plumber, carpenter, farrier, and many others might be needed (just like now and throughout the past). Learning a skill as a hobby now might turn out to be very valuable knowledge at some future time.

Many items that are cheap now could be very valuable in a long-term situation. A simple cigarette lighter can be bought three for a dollar now but would be impossible for a regular guy to make. I cannot make matches, but I can certainly store up some matches.

In a long-term situation, a simple small cut could easily cause your death through infection. Having antibiotic cream or some hydrogen peroxide on hand could save your life or the life of a loved one. Many folks store animal antibiotics to use on themselves in a future situation. Antibiotics used for fish or livestock or pets are often the exact same thing as your doctor uses now on you. Same with bandages; the ones used for pets are just as sterile as the ones in the emergency room at the hospital. Many native wild plants offer antibiotic properties, learn about them.

Many talk about 'operational security.' I touched on this earlier as it means keeping quiet about your preps. If you have to tell someone about the neat prep thing you just bought then tell your grandma who lives two thousand miles away. Do not tell your neighbor or all the people you work with about everything you do to prepare. If you tell everyone then if/when something bad happens they will all show up at your door. And they will not come alone; they will bring their friends and extended family. It bears repeating – 'Loose lips sink ships.'

A 22 caliber rifle is an excellent tool for harvesting small game. The longer the barrel, the quieter it will be. There is special ammunition like "Quiet Ammo' that is made by CCI. This is reduced powder charge ammunition that is quieter than standard ammo (and obviously with less power). It will not operate a semi-automatic rifle (can be shot as a single shot but not very practical) but will work fine in a bolt action, lever action, or other manual action rifle.

In a bad situation always think quiet and concealment. Stealth is your friend in any bad situation. Be quiet and be inconspicuous. Have camouflage clothing or at least drab earth tone colors. Movement and noise will draw attention to you when you are outside, and this can be a bad thing. You are much harder to see if you are in the shade rather than in the sun. Learn how to use obstructions for concealment and learn how to leave fewer tracks and signs of your passage. Use different routes and times to confuse and evade possible attackers.

Quality binoculars allow you to see many things that you would not see otherwise. They are invaluable both for security reasons and for hunting or scouting.

Communications during/after a disaster are questionable. In many cases, your cell phone may very well not be working. If the power grid is down the cell towers will be down shortly after (from immediately to one or two days). Even if the power is still on often circuits will be jammed from all the calls.

Or your government has the power to shut off all phone usage (they are always listening to your calls already). You can purchase your own two-way radios for your family to use. The makers of the radios lie totally about the range of their radios. Common, inexpensive radios like FRS / GMRS radios are sometimes touted to have a range of twenty miles (or even more) while in practical use the range is more like ¼ to ½ mile. This can actually be a blessing in some cases because the calls can be monitored by anyone but because the range is so short, they would at least have to be very close to monitor your calls.

Everyone should include a battery-powered radio in their preps. Or even better a crank up and/or solar powered radio. These are relatively inexpensive ($20 to $50) and will allow you to listen to normal AM/FM radio stations in your area during a disaster situation. Some have the 'weather band' to allow you to hear dedicated weather reports or alerts for your area. The radio can give moral support just by having it on and provide vital local information along with government propaganda.

Fire can certainly be your friend in survival situations. Every family member should be trained how to start a fire using different methods. Matches, cigarette lighters, magnifying glass, Ferro rod, magnesium starters, and flint & steel are some of the common fire starting methods.

Everyone should know you need 'tinder' to start a fire. Tinder is some easily combustible material used to help start a fire. Examples of common tinder are a newspaper, dryer lint, steel wool, dry grass, dry leaves, or most any light dry burnable material. Once it starts to burn then increasingly larger burnable material is gradually added until you have a fire the size you desire. This might be a huge bonfire as a signal or a tiny fire just to boil a cup of water.

A small candle can be a big help when trying to start a fire and candles are an inexpensive prep item anyway to provide light, heat, and moral comfort.

Fire can also be a serious enemy. Do not start your large campfire under a tree with branches above your fire. You should have trees and brush cut way back from your house if at all possible to prevent a wildfire from taking your house with it. This is the same advice that fire departments say now and will be even more important in a bad situation. Clearing the area around your home has the added benefit of removing hiding spots for attackers and opening up your fields of fire.

I am not a big knife fan, but they are a very necessary and vital prep item. Their uses are countless, and so are their models, styles, sizes, and prices. In my opinion, the models with blades longer than six inches or so have somewhat limited value. If I need something bigger then likely a good hatchet will work better anyway. An exception would be a good machete to trim brush. A good pocket knife along with a good belt knife is a fine choice to carry. For a belt knife either a good quality folder with maybe a four-inch blade or better yet a fixed blade belt knife with a four or five-inch blade. A quality knife does not have to cost over a hundred dollars, but it will cost more than the five dollar ones that are often found at flea markets and such.

Yes, big heavy knives have valid uses. But they are also heavy and bulky if you will be carrying them. Everything is always a trade-off.

A knife is almost worthless and can cause accidents if it is not sharp. Any tool you have that is designed to be sharp should be kept in that condition at all times. Sharpeners are like knives in all the different styles that are available. Diamond sharpeners are a good choice, but there are many other good choices. Learn to sharpen your own tools now while the world is in good shape. Not after the world has fallen and your very life may depend on your ability to maintain your equipment.

Propane can be stored just about forever. Propane can be fuel for everything from your pickup and generator to your kitchen stove and refrigerator. In many cases, propane appliances require no electricity to operate so are great for grid-down situations. Propane can heat your home, cook your food, and freeze your butchered deer all without any electric power.

The only real downside to propane is that you can not make it yourself so in an extended long-term event what you have on hand is all you will ever have. I personally think propane is an excellent choice for a kitchen range. You can easily store enough propane to run that range for a very long time. Other fuels might be better for other things, but it is hard to beat a propane powered range in a grid down scenario whether it is a short term or long term (as long as you have some propane stored). It can cook your food and heat at least part of your home.

Some people believe that if they see birds and animals drink or eat something that it is perfectly safe for them to eat or drink that also. This is NOT true. Obviously, it can be true at times but certainly not always. Know what you are eating or leave it alone. Boil your water!

Those of you that live in large cities know that getting out during or after a disaster could be a nightmare or even impossible. Plan ahead for what you will do. If your plan is to evacuate then have multiple routes planned and checked out ahead of time then leave early if at all possible. If you plan to stay do your planning around the fact that you will 'shelter in place.' But always have a backup plan or two, and one of them should be an evacuation.

What about a BOB? A bug out bag. These are talked about everywhere. I have gear in every vehicle to help me get home safely in an emergency (like a GHB=get home bag). That gear would also help me if I had to leave home quickly and took a vehicle. But I do not have a BOB per say.

I can see the advantage of having a pack set up and ready to go at all times. I also have my RV always ready to go at a moments notice containing plenty of gear and food. If you want and need to have a BOB, then that is a good choice for you.

The list of contents of a BOB varies with everyone, and many examples can be found on the internet (even pre-loaded ones to buy). Always remember the chapters of this book when packing – water, food, shelter, and security and then pack accordingly. Have a BOB for each member of your family if you wish. Your six year old can certainly have a small pack with their personal things in it.

In your BOB, food and water are obvious choices to add. A method of getting more potable water is a good idea and would mean packing a compact water filter and/or even a small cooking pot that you could use to boil water (and cook in). Shelter could be a tent or just a tarp. Security could be a gun, knife, hatchet, or even a hammer depending on local laws and what you own (a cane or walking stick can be a fair defensive tool).

Logical other items like two or more ways to start a fire, medications (include aspirin or similar), spare clothes, cash, maps, GPS (?), binoculars, and some cordage. Other items as you see fit.

But remember you have to carry all this stuff so keep the weight to a minimum. If you have children, your BOB will be packed way different than if you are a single male. Having a pack ready to go might be a good idea but so is having a destination picked out to go to also.

Many people talk about 'bugging out to the hills', and that is their total destination. That is fine, but it would make more sense to have several spots picked out and scouted ahead of time. You would need more than one spot as I assume you would not own the land and it likely would be public land which could easily be occupied by others when you get there.

So your 'favorite' spot might have many people there when you arrive. If your plan then is to 'live off the land' that is still maybe feasible but pretty unlikely even if you have the needed training. In the beginning, you could likely get meat by hunting small game but what about something other than meat to eat?

You might be planning shooting big game, but if the temperature is above freezing, it will spoil quickly. It could be dried, jerked, or canned to preserve it but do you have the equipment and know-how to do that? Shooting more big game every couple days because the meat spoils quickly is a very poor plan.

Even if you have a couple of good books on edible plants in your area that does not mean you will find anything to eat. Many edible plants are only good to eat at certain times of the year and often only one part of the plant is edible (leaves, roots, fruits, flowers). Certainly, if your plan involves harvesting and eating wild plants, you should practice that before you need to depend on it. It would also mean always being on the move to forage on wild plants. When foraging the rule of thumb is only to take some and leave some so the source will grow back so it can be harvested again and again. If you watch wild game that is how they eat. They eat some and move on then stop and eat more before again moving. That way they do not destroy their whole food source at just that one time.

I have eaten many, many wild plants and try different ones as I find them. Some taste excellent and some I have spit out as fast as I could. Many wild berries are equal or better than any stuff you can buy (maybe choke cherries not so much!). Many wild edible plants have very little taste and could do with some embellishment. Many wild plants have very little nutritional value. And you would likely expend more calories gathering some of them than they provide.

An excellent light and inexpensive item to have is a tea ball to hold tea leaves. These are often made of aluminum or stainless steel, and you can hook it to your pack when hiking. Then when you see a plant that is good for making a 'wild' tea you can pick it and stuff it in your tea ball for future use. It is also useful at home as many find tea (or use it with coffee to make a single cup) to be nicer to drink than plain water and a hot beverage can help you keep warm in a cold environment and be a great morale booster.

Dry drink mixes are also an excellent prep item to store. They keep a very long time and can be used as a treat for kids or adults. Many also contain some vitamins, especially vitamin C. Even in your BOB they make that filtered water taste much better. Just because the water is filtered or boiled and safe to drink does not mean that it is going to taste good. Pond water will still likely taste like pond water.

Multi-vitamins are a good prep item. Your eating habits will likely change, and you might end up missing some essential vitamins and taking one a day could make a big difference in your long-term health and that of your family.

If you are or plan on being sexually active, you might want to prep some contraceptives or some baby supplies. And maybe a how-to book on having a baby when away from a hospital. I assume it is pretty easy because people have been having babies for several years now.

Electronic devices do not have to die if the power grid goes down if you plan ahead a little. There are many small solar chargers for things like smart phones, I-pads, I-pods, laptops, kindles, or for charging regular rechargeable batteries like AA's.

We have all seen those solar lawn lights and they often only cost only a couple of dollars each. Most contain a double A rechargeable battery, and it has a built-in solar charger. You can use the charged batteries from those lights in your other items. The solar lights can also be used as a rechargeable flashlight.

Solar panels have come way down in price and are much more common now. They can often be found used for big cost savings. Smaller ones new are maybe about two dollars a watt, and large ones are about a dollar a watt. Many mount solar panels on top of their RV's to charge their batteries to run many appliances and lights.

They can be purchased and mounted on your house or outbuildings or even just laid on the ground. A few hundred watts of solar and a couple of deep cycle batteries with a power inverter can run a small refrigerator/freezer, and some LED lights. There are many examples of making a portable solar rig on the internet also. Sometimes these are called a solar generator.

A solar setup is very simple and only has four parts. Solar panel or panels, a solar charge controller, one or more batteries, and a power inverter to change the DC power to AC (house) power. This is not rocket science. Each solar panel has two wires, a plus+ and a minus-. The solar charge controller will be clearly marked for what wire goes where + or -. Each battery will have two terminals that are clearly marked plus+ and minus-. The power inverter will have the terminals clearly marked for plus+ and minus-.

Many people store their long-term food items in five-gallon buckets. If the food comes into contact with the bucket, then you should make sure the bucket is made of 'food-safe' plastic. These buckets can often be purchased used for free or at low cost from bakeries or delis or other food prep places. Or you can buy new food safe buckets from many different stores, even Home Depot.

The five-gallon buckets do stack nicely when full (or empty) and do have a handy bail handle to move them. They seal out moisture and vermin. Also, empty juice containers or other plastic or glass containers can be washed out and re-used that will cost you nothing.

These containers make excellent moisture and vermin proof storage containers. Use them for rice, beans, wheat, pasta, or whatever will fit in them. That empty glass food jar can be used to store matches, both wooden matches and book matches (most casinos give out free book matches which are an excellent prep item). If you have many of a certain size container, then make your shelving to fit that container for the least loss of space.

Another prep item that is often forgotten is boots and shoes. In the cold climate areas, you will want to have high-quality well-insulated boots to wear in the winter. For summer wear or in warm climates leather work boots and leather hikers are good choices. If you are prepping for kids, you have to guess about larger sizes for future wear.

For those who are prepping that are overweight, you might find that weight loss will come with a long-term event, and your current clothes might no longer fit very well. Of course, that is why your belt has more notches, isn't it? And oversize clothes can still be used way easier than undersize ones.

Sewage has to be thought about before any event. Loss of power will mean the loss of sewage pumps so raw sewage could overflow into your home or apartment (if in a city). Even those in the country often have septic systems that have a lift pump and when that lift pump stops the tank will overflow at some point.

Floods can also cause raw sewage to overflow. Besides being a smelly mess, there is an obvious health risk. Plus you still have to go somewhere. Short term solutions can be a porta-potty like for camping or even just a bucket and some dry kitty litter.

If you are on a 'city' sewer system and live on a hill, you might have no problem at all as everything will flow downhill to someone else's house. If you are on a second or third floor or higher apartment, you will likely have no problem inside your apartment, but soon the smell will rise from below (and from the street outside). In many cases, this sewage problem will require your evacuation, and you will actually be anxious to leave that area.

In the rural areas, a simple outhouse can be the answer or some home septic systems have no pumps and will function just fine without any electricity. In many cases, this raw sewage problem will contaminate the local water supply. Nearby rivers, lakes, or ponds will be contaminated quickly and make getting fresh water a serious problem.

In bad disaster situations, city dwellers can face many severe hardships that rural folks might not. And some disasters (like riots) will only directly affect those that live in the city. Security in the city is also a serious problem especially with commonly more restrictions placed on those that live there when it comes to defensive items.

In some or even most situations sheltering in place may still be a viable option but in many cases leaving is the only good option. If you live in an urban area, have a plan for both staying and going.

We all might have to evacuate our homes for many different reasons, and that reason could come up with no prior warning. Keep fuel in your vehicles at all times. When you get down to three-quarter tank or so stop and fill the tank. How long does it take, five minutes? Are you that tied up that you don't have five minutes you can spare in a week or even every few days? Can you still live if you miss five minutes of 'Dancing with the Stars' just to always have a full tank of fuel in your vehicle?

Stored prep items should include things to pass the time and provide mental comfort. Games, books (including fiction books), candy, coloring books, and crayons; things like these can boost everyone's morale and should be stored as prep items. Most alcoholic drinks can be stored a long time and have many possible uses. Just another prep item that while not vital is a multi-use item.

Some appliances are just about designed for preppers. Dehydrators have been around for years and work great to dry many things for preppers to store. A dehydrator is a great investment. If you have kids and want them to eat healthy snacks just dehydrate some apple or other fruits and your kids will likely love them.

A vacuum sealer works great for your dehydrated food and also many other things. If you vacuum seal some clothes for in your BOB, they will take up way less room and be clean and dry when you open them. Also, you can get an attachment for the vac sealer to do jars. So you can store more stuff for longer periods by vacuum sealing it in jars (like all that food you ran through the dehydrator).

A crock pot can cook many things while you are free to do other chores and they use less electric power so can possibly run one using your solar generator (maybe).

A hand meat grinder could be used now to provide less expensive lean hamburger. Buy an inexpensive roast when it is on sale for less per pound than lean hamburger and then grind it yourself at home.

Did you cook a roast or steak that was too tough even to eat? Use your hand meat grinder and then use that formally tough meat for sandwiches or on top of your pizza or whatever, run it through your hand grinder, and it will no longer be tough. After you have picked, soaked, and shelled your acorns you can then run them through your meat grinder to grind them into meal that you can use to make a version of pancakes! These listed small appliances are often seen at yard sales and in thrift stores at a fraction of the new price.

Try making your own jerky at home. You can use your oven or a dehydrator. Almost everyone likes jerky, and it is a healthy snack that does not need refrigeration. There are hundreds of recipes online. Try a couple of different recipes then alter them to fit your personal tastes. Once you make jerky, you will then know a way to preserve meat that does not require a freezer!

In a long-term situation, there will likely be a lot of competition for the limited food available. Besides humans, this competition will include all the other carnivores in the area. Cats, dogs, coyotes, wolves, bears, raccoons, owls, hawks, eagles and more will all be trying to eat the same stuff that you are, like that tasty looking bunny in the front yard.

The obvious thing for you to do is thin this competition out as much as you can so there is more food for you. Kill these animals and eat them if possible to get back some of the protein that they have already taken from you. If you are raising a garden or chickens or rabbits for food, any of these creatures can devastate your food supply. Kill them with guns or traps or snares. If given a chance they would likely eat you too.

Epilogue

I hope you have received some benefit from reading this short book. Like stated earlier so many people have such different circumstances that you have to modify things listed in here to fit your specific needs and many of the things listed may be of no use you at all.

At least by reading this book, you have acknowledged the need to be prepared for what might be in your future.   Even if you never have to suffer the effects of a disaster, you can still receive benefits from many things listed in this book.

The End

I hope you enjoyed this short guide and invite you to read some of the following fiction stories that I have already published. All are found on Kindle, and most are also available in print. I now have well over sixty titles from which to choose.

Thank you for reading this guide.

Pete Thorsen

No Electric Survival

This is a story of the aftermath of a severe EMP that shuts down the nation's electric power grid and makes most vehicles unusable. Naturally, this leads to devastating consequences for everyone. This story follows a group of friends and family as they band together to try to survive in a whole new world without electricity.

This is the first story I ever wrote. I published it on a whim. Its immediate popularity was amazing and prompted me to continue writing.

Pandemic to New Beginning

This is a story that follows the lives of two twenty-somethings before and after a deadly flu pandemic sweeps around the globe causing a severe drop in the world population. Those that survive the pandemic soon find that their troubles are only just now beginning.

Rural Dollar Collapse

This story takes place in two widely separated rural areas in the United States. When there is a complete collapse of the American Dollar and the resulting collapse of the US economy this story shows how members of one family cope with what happens in their areas of the once great United States.

No Economic Collapse

In the Woods

This is a story of troubled economic times in the United States that ends in total economic collapse and the resulting chaos. The story centers on three people that are strangers to each other but find strength when circumstances throw them together and they try to live their lives in the bleak new world they now have to survive in.

The Carrington Event Revisited

This is the story of a catastrophic solar coronal mass ejection event similar to the one that hit the Earth in 1859. This story follows a man trying to survive in a world that is much harsher than the one he grew up in but one in which he is determined to overcome despite all obstacles.

A Collapse to a
Fresh Start

This is a story of two young people who make their way out of Chicago and run to a very rural area of Colorado when they feel the United States is about to suffer an economic collapse and maybe change forever. The change both for them and in their country is a very large one indeed.

A Midwest Homestead

This story follows the lives of a young couple in Minnesota who through determination and hard work build their own little homestead in the country. A homestead that ultimately is their salvation in a time chaos.

An Oklahoma Retreat

This is the story of a widely scattered family that all return to the original family ranch in Oklahoma when the United States falls on very bad times. This is their story of how they all planned ahead and then worked together to make it through those troubled times. The very real power of family ties helps them all while trying to keep their humanity through some very dark times.

An Arizona Haven

This story takes place in Arizona after an EMP or CME has shut down the whole power grid and rendered most vehicles inoperable. Centered around a man who when this event happens is trapped in a place with no home and no friends who eventually finds both along with a lot of pain and heartbreak along the way. It is a story of how a will to overcome obstacles and some common sense can mean all the difference in your very survival.

Dystopia USA

This story is the tale of a possible dark future in the great United States of America. It is not a bright future that is filled with promise but an ugly future that is only filled with despair. It follows three different groups of characters in different areas of the country and with different backgrounds. Each has their own trials and tribulations as this once great nation changes in dramatic and disconcerting ways.

Note: This story is dark and far from being uplifting. It gives a very bleak look into a possible future that none of us would want.

The Zombie Plague

This is a story of a Zombie plague that is affecting the whole world. In this story, the 'zombies' are not the 'un-dead' but are cannibalistic simple-minded creatures that were once human but have been changed forever. This story is centered around a small number of dedicated people and starts at the beginning of the plague and follows its spread around the globe while every scientist and doctor around the world races to find a cure.

How I Survived WW3

This is a story that follows a regular working man that happens to survive World War Three after making just a few low-cost preparations that fit his limited budget. He tells the story of how he survived and what happens to him in the aftermath as he lives through the 'nuclear winter' that follows.

Living Through the Collapse

This story is about the economic collapse of the US Dollar and the economy of the USA as lived through by a family in rural Minnesota. Naturally, in the troubled times they face some hardships and do suffer a crippling loss, but the family survives and perseveres through whatever is thrown at them. They totally rely on each other, and their family bond is strong.

Polar Shift

This story is about two good friends and their lives before and after a major catastrophic event. When a fairly large metallic asteroid passes by very closely to the earth, it triggers a spontaneous 'geomagnetic reversal.' This causes untold havoc throughout the whole world. The world is quickly turned into a totally different place where survival is the only thing on everyone's mind.

America on Fire

Four complete stories of apocalyptic disasters that befall the citizens of the United States by one of America's popular apocalyptic fiction writers. Read how some Americans rise up to meet the challenges and fight to survive when disaster strikes.

In **Finding Hope** a deadly pandemic sweeps the globe resulting in the deaths of a large amount of the world population. One man finds a purpose to his life when he finds and befriends a little girl.

In **Three Strikes And You're Out America** three nuclear EMP missiles explode high above the United States it causes extreme devastation by taking out the whole electric grid and all electronics.

In **An Economic Firestorm,** the economic collapse of the US Dollar and the economy of the USA are lived through by a family in rural Arizona.

In **Thar, She Blows** see what happens to a few groups of people when the Yellowstone Caldera erupts and devastates a huge portion of the United States.

Disaster in America

Four complete stories of apocalyptic disasters that befall the citizens of the United States by one of America's most popular apocalyptic fiction writers. Read how some Americans rise up to meet the challenges and fight to survive when disaster strikes.

In **What? The sun did all this!** A massively strong CME that strikes the earth destroying the electric grid and most electric devices. One man attempts to reunite with his scattered family.

In **Surviving in Trying Times** one middle-aged couple trying to cope with what becomes something like the second great depression.

In **Relax It's Just the Flu** a massive pandemic of a deadly strain of the flu wreaks havoc on the USA. This story follows a few of the survivors.

In **Global Warming (It's real this time)** a young man struggles to survive twenty years after a man-made accident actually does cause massive global warming.

A Girl's Gotta Survive

In a little different twist from my other books, this story is about a young woman. Told in her own words, it follows the trials and tribulations she has faced in her life from an early age. Just when it seems she has a handle on things and it looks like a brighter future may be in front of her the nation's economy falls into serious decline. This, of course, causes problems for our heroine but also for the whole nation. But she is a fighter with a serious will to survive. Will she succeed?

After The Second Great Depression

The second Great Depression came about from many factors. The non-existence of a recovery from the recession of two thousand eight, the war with the Islamic State, the bungling actions of the Federal Reserve Bank, and when things got worse the last straw was the declaration of Martial Law here in the United States. This story is not about any of those events. This story is about one man who lived through those events and the many years following the Second Great Depression. Now eight years later the United States is a very different place. It is a harsh place where everyone must be strong to survive, and everyone has to rely just on themselves for their survival.

Stormy Weather

Following the Great Recession of 2009, the United States enjoyed several years of economic 'recovery.' At least that is what our government and the media kept telling the nation's population. Chip, a construction worker in Nebraska, was not too sure about the whole economic recovery thing. He never really saw too much improvement where he was living and working.

Then things really started to go downhill with the nation's economy. It just kept getting worse and worse, and soon even the media could no longer hide the truth that this time the fake recovery was turning into the Second Great Depression.

Chip still had the old farmstead that had been passed down through several generations in his family. Could he make a go of it on only the small piece of that land that was still left? He knew he would have to use all the old knowledge that his parents had passed to him just to keep his belly full in this new depression with even longer 'soup lines' than there was in the first Great Depression. Chip never said he was the brightest bulb, but even he knew the nation was in for some stormy weather.

This is his story.

Bound for Home

While traveling for work a man finds himself almost two thousand miles from home when a terrorist attack cripples the whole system infrastructure across the United States. His one and only thought after this event is to get home to his wife as quickly as possible. The man encounters personal hardships during this trip back home, but he will let nothing stop him from achieving his one goal of reuniting with the one he loves.

Minnesota Madness, A series of large earthquakes in widespread areas, proves to be just a

warning for one twenty-four hour period of massive earthquakes that damage many countries around the world. This included the New Madrid Seismic Zone in the center of America. While suffering no physical damage from the many quakes Minnesota falls apart from the repercussions of the devastation. A single man makes plans for his own survival after the madness strikes.

House on the Hill   Lucas built the house of his

dreams and was determined to stay there alone and have as little contact with other people as possible. Lucas thought troubling times were ahead and that played a big part in the house design and the location he picked for it. He just hoped if something did happen he could just stay home and ride it out, alone.

Ruination of America

Three complete stories of apocalyptic disasters that befall the citizens of the United States by one of America's most popular apocalyptic fiction writers. Read how some Americans rise to meet the challenges and fight to survive when disaster strikes.

The Lottery Winner. When Jake wins the lottery, it changes his life. And his life needs changing too as a somewhat screwed up veteran. He starts to get his head on straight and then the nation's economy starts to crumble. As things get worse and worse, Jake tries to think of ways to stay ahead of the game.

Cincinnati Shutdown. This is a story of a teenager becoming a man over several years during increasingly bad economic times in the city of Cincinnati. When the economy completely falls apart, is he man enough to protect those he loves?

Korean Chaos. Lars and his family feel safe in their rural house in the middle of America. But with North Korea constantly threatening the United States and now knowing that Korea does have long-range ICBM's and the nukes to fit them, things seem much more serious. So together the married couple decides to take a few precautions for 'just in case.' The question is, have they done enough and done it soon enough? Can they protect their young daughter if something does happen?

Hope for America?

Three complete stories of apocalyptic disasters that befall the citizens of the United States by one of America's most popular apocalyptic fiction writers. Read how some Americans rise to meet the challenges and fight to survive when disaster strikes.

Trouble In Texas   A drifter who stops near a Texas city and decides to stay, at least for awhile. And that's where he finds himself when a deadly pandemic sweeps across the globe. Texas is not spared, and this one man does what he can to survive the deadly disease. The disease kills hundreds of millions of people around the world, will this one man survive? Will he even want to survive when so many others are dead?

Canadian Adventure   Shortly after arriving in Canada for their Dad's new job these two teenagers are kidnapped and through a series of events wind up crash landed alone in the Canadian wilderness. But the kids take it in stride and make the most of what they have to work with to survive in the dire situation where they now find themselves. They make it through every day with only the hope of rescue to keep them going.

Mountain Hideaway   A man is lucky enough to find the love of his life and marries her. He now thinks he has everything he has ever wanted and then the whole world around him collapses. The economy falls apart, and no one knows what to do about it as it gets worse and worse. He and his wife live in his dream location in the mountains. Is their house remote enough to keep them safe as the world descends into complete chaos?